THE ROUGH GUIDE TO
Keyboards
& Digital Piano

Written by

Hugo Pinksterboer

ROUGH
GUIDES

THE ESSENTIAL TIPBOOK

Rough Guide Tipbook Credits

Journalist, writer and musician **Hugo Pinksterboer** has written hundreds of articles and reviews for international music magazines. He is the author of the reference work for cymbals (*The Cymbal Book*, Hal Leonard, US) and has written and developed a wide variety of musical manuals and courses.

Illustrator, designer and musician **Gijs Bierenbroodspot** has worked as an art director in magazines and advertising. While searching in vain for information about saxophone mouthpieces he came up with the idea for this series of books on music and musical instruments. Since then, he has created the layout and the illustrations for all of the books.

Acknowledgements

Concept, design and illustrations: Gijs Bierenbroodspot

Translation: MdJ Copy & Translation

Editor: Kim Burton

IN BRIEF

Are you just starting to play a keyboard instrument, or planning to buy a home keyboard or digital piano? Or just trying to get the best out of an instrument you already own? Read on. This Tipbook is for everyone wanting to know what really matters about home keyboards and digital pianos.

All the facts
Once you've read this book, you'll be able to get the best out of your instrument, make informed purchases, and understand pretty much all the jargon you'll come across in magazines and brochures. It tells you everything you need to know, instead of everything there is to know. It will also stay up to date for a long, long time, as it concerns itself with the basics.

Skipping the first four chapters
The first four chapters have been written for first-time buyers and players. If you're more advanced you may skip them and fast forward to chapter 5 or any of the other chapters.

Glossary
The glossary at the end of the book briefly explains most of the terms you'll come across as a keyboard player and it doubles as an index.

CONTENTS

1. A KEYBOARD PLAYER?

Home keyboards, digital pianos and other keyboard instruments have one thing in common: the keyboard, of course. So if you play any of these instruments, you're a keyboard player. Keyboards are versatile enough to be used for solo and ensemble playing.

And keyboard players can be prominent band leaders as well as dimly lit sidemen, playing either a single piano, operating huge multiple keyboard stacks, or anything in between.

Keyboard instruments (*keys*, for short) are different from most other instruments in that you can play a solo and take care of the accompaniment at the same time, playing chords with your left hand. Both home keyboards and pianos can be used for pretty much any style of music. In fact, it's only in classical music that home keyboards are somewhat out of place.

The band

Home keyboards differ from pianos because they have built-in *accompaniments* that can take on the combined roles of drummer, bass player, pianist, guitarist, and even brass and string sections. At quite a number of parties or functions the entire 'band' is just one person playing a professional home keyboard.

Of course, there's nothing to stop you from using a keyboard in a band, either. With the accompaniments switched off, it can just as easily be used to play string parts, flute counter-melodies, trumpet or piano solos, or whatever else you like.

1

Band leaders

Keyboard players are important members of the band, not only because of what they play, but because they often double as musical directors. Keyboard players, having an ear for both melody and harmony (how notes sound together), are often faster at working tunes out by ear than other musicians, and are more likely to write their own, too.

EVEN BETTER

Here are a few more advantages to playing keyboards.

- On a keyboard, every note has its own key. You want a higher note? Move to the right. Want a lower one? Move to the left. That's about as easy as it can be.
- Learning to play a keyboard instrument well takes just as long as learning any other instrument. But it won't take you that long to play something that sounds acceptable. Certainly not as long as it would on a violin or a trumpet. On a home keyboard you may produce something quite impressive sounding within just a few weeks.
- Home keyboards start at very friendly prices, and digital pianos are generally cheaper than acoustic ones.
- Most instruments have amps and speakers built in, so there's no need to buy them as extras.
- Just plug in your headphones, and you can play in the middle of the night. Without disturbing the neighbours.

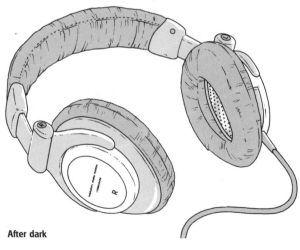

After dark

- Home keyboards are very portable, weighing a maximum of about twenty pounds. Granted, digital pianos are a good deal heavier, but have you ever tried lifting an acoustic one?

What's in a name?

Home keyboards and digital pianos (or *home pianos*, as they are also known) share one annoying feature: their names are a bit too long. So from now on, the words 'home' and 'digital' may be left out from time to time.

Impracticalities

Different manufacturers tend to use different names for similar features. For example, many names are used to indicate the auto-accompaniment section, ranging from *conductor* to *style*. It's as impractical as it is impossible to list every single name that may be used for every feature, so usually one or two typical examples are given.

Warning

Unless you like making enemies, never call anyone who plays an acoustic piano without recourse to speakers, amplifiers and leads/cables a keyboard player.

2. A QUICK TOUR

All those buttons, sliders, levers and connections make home keyboards look more complicated than they really are. Pianos are quite a bit easier on the eye. Here's a quick tour to take the mystery out of both, introducing the main similarities as well as the main differences.

The main thing these instruments have in common is of course the keyboard. Many digital pianos have as many keys as acoustic ones (normally 88), while others come with 76. Home keyboards usually have fewer keys. If you're serious about playing, then go for one with at least 61 keys.

61-note keyboard (GEM)

Sounds

Most home keyboards have well over a hundred different sounds, ranging from acoustic guitars to organs, goblins and telephones. Pianos often have only five to ten sounds, including a few acoustic and electric pianos, organ and vibes. Strings and choirs are popular extra sounds.

Samples
For each sound, one or more *samples* are used: little pre-recorded snippets, digitally stored on microchips. Hit a key, and a sample is 'retranslated' back into a sound.

Band-in-a-box
In effect, a home keyboard is a band-in-a-box, with a built-in drummer, a bass player and a host of other electronic musicians. Just hit a key on the keyboard, and an entire orchestra starts playing for you. Most styles of music are catered for – rock, waltz, jazz, hard-core, country, techno, dance; you name it. Some pianos have built-in accompaniments too. They are often called *rhythm pianos*.

Two more differences
The home keyboard stems from the organ. Digital pianos stem from the acoustic piano. Organ playing is quite different from piano playing: the keys are pressed rather than struck, and the sound sustains as long as they're held down. On a piano the sound always dies away after a short while.

Why a piano?
Home keyboards invariably have at least a couple of piano sounds on board. So why bother buying a digital piano? The answer, in short, is the quality of the sound. Digital pianos have fewer options and on average cost more than home keyboards, but they have higher-quality samples, more samples per sound, superior amplifiers and more powerful speakers, so they sound more like real pianos.

Weighted action
Digital pianos *feel* more like acoustic ones, too. They have special keyboards that mimic the action of hammers hitting strings, which is what happens when you play an acoustic piano.

Four types
There are roughly four different types of digital piano. The first type has only a basic set of piano sounds as mentioned above. The second type has many more sounds, and includes accompaniments. The third type is the *stage piano*, which is intended for use on stage rather than in the living room. Designed to be lugged around, stage pianos

tend to be encased in metal rather than wood, and they don't always have internal speakers. Finally, there are acoustic pianos and grand pianos with built-in digital facilities, offering both the playing and sound characteristics of a 'real' piano and the advantages of a digital instrument, such as a number of sampled sounds and facilities for silent practice.

WHAT EVERYTHING DOES

Home keyboards and digital pianos are not really that complicated, once you get to know them. Here's a quick tour of the main features and controls. The illustrations show you where everything is located on a typical instrument.

Selecting sounds and accompaniments

Sound selection on pianos is usually a matter of pushing the button with the name of the sound you're looking for. That doesn't work on a keyboard, of course; there's just no room for hundreds of dedicated buttons. So instead, sounds (also referred to as *voices* or *tones*) are selected by punching in a number on a keypad, or by choosing an option from the *display*. The accompaniments are selected in much the same way.

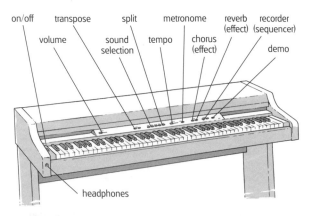

Digital piano (Yamaha)

Selecting sounds on a digital piano

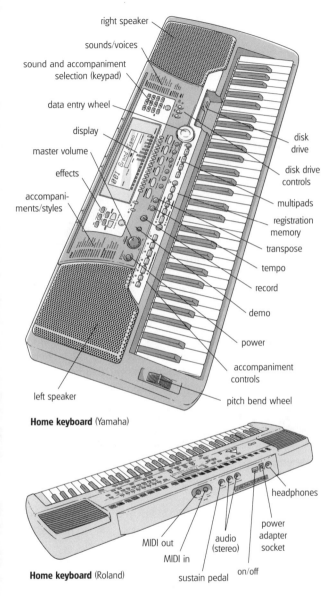

right speaker

sounds/voices

sound and accompaniment
selection (keypad)

data entry wheel

display

master volume

effects

accompani-
ments/styles

left speaker

disk
drive

disk drive
controls

multipads

registration
memory

transpose

tempo

record

demo

power

accompaniment
controls

pitch bend wheel

Home keyboard (Yamaha)

headphones

MIDI out

MIDI in

audio
(stereo)

sustain pedal

on/off

power
adapter
socket

Home keyboard (Roland)

Start, stop and in-between

In addition to start and stop buttons for the accompaniment, there are controls for adding an *intro* or an *ending*
to a song, for varying the basic accompaniment pattern or
style, and for inserting *fills* or *fill-ins* (short variations
between two sections of a song).

Chords

The only way to play chords (three or more notes at a time) on a piano is to actually hit all the right notes. Home keyboards have simpler ways of playing chords; you can choose whether you want to play them using just one finger, two fingers, or the whole handful.

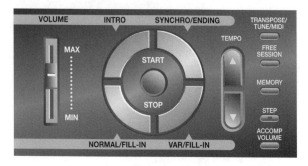

Accompaniment controls: start, stop, fill-in, variation

Tempo

With a pair of up/down buttons you can set the tempo (speed) for the orchestra. Pianos usually have similar buttons which control a built-in metronome that produces a click or short beep to help you to keep steady time.

Metronome controls (left)

What you see...

A display shows you which sounds and accompaniments you have selected. Most instruments go way beyond that, also displaying among other things tempo, the keys you are pressing and the bar/measure you're in – so you always know where you are and what you're doing. Pianos have rather basic displays, or none at all.

... and what you hear

On keyboards, the speakers are often in full view, sitting behind a speaker grille. On pianos they're usually hidden away somewhere. Amplification is taken care of by a built-in stereo amplifier.

Loud and soft

Most keyboards and all pianos have *touch-sensitive* keyboards; the harder you hit a key, the louder the sound will be. The instrument's overall volume is set with a volume control. Keyboards often allow you to control the volume with your foot, by using a *volume* or *expression pedal.*

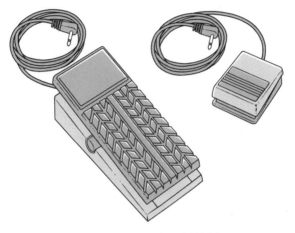

Volume or expression pedal, and sustain pedal (right)

Pianos and pedals

Acoustic pianos have two or three pedals; most digital ones have two. The one on the right is the most important one; it's the *sustain pedal*, which lets the sound ring out freely after you release the keys. The left pedal is the *soft pedal*, and that describes its effect quite clearly. It's also known as the *piano pedal*; 'piano' is Italian for soft.

Pedals for keyboards

Apart from the volume and sustain pedals mentioned above, other kinds of pedals can be used with keyboards; footswitches which start or stop the accompaniment, for instance.

Split

 With a *split* feature you can divide the keyboard into two or more sections, allowing you to play a different sound in each section. This feature is most commonly found on keyboards, but may be available on pianos as well.

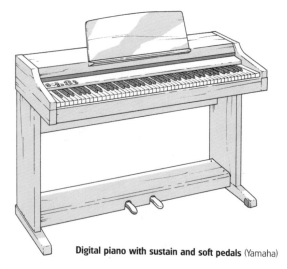

Digital piano with sustain and soft pedals (Yamaha)

Layer

If you want to blend, say, the sound of a guitar with that of a group of violins, you can do so by simply stacking these sounds on top of each other. On most keyboards this option is called *layering*, but you may also come across names such as *dual voice*. Some pianos have this feature too.

Pads

Most keyboards have a special set of *touch keys* or (*multi-*) *pads* that can trigger drum sounds or sound effects.

Bass drums and triangles

On many keyboards you can use the keys to play a host of percussion instruments. Each key triggers one sound from

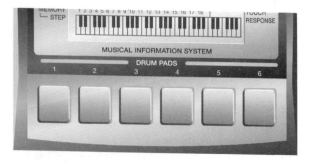

Six pads with dedicated drum sounds (Casio)

a range that stretches from a bass drum to a triangle or a conga. The more sophisticated home keyboards allow you to store the rhythms that you create.

The mix

When you have several sounds playing at once, using layers, splits and accompaniments, it's useful to be able to set the volume of each sound separately. In professional language this is called setting the mix.

TWEAKING THE SOUNDS

Both keyboards and pianos have fixed *preset sounds* that you cannot modify extensively, as you can on synthesizers. However, most instruments do feature effects like reverb, delay and chorusing, and some keyboards offer basic editing possibilities similar to those found on synthesizers.

Reverb

One of the most popular built-in effects is *reverb*. Using reverb makes your instrument sound as if you're playing in a big hall, or in a church or even a cathedral instead of at home. Another popular effect is *chorus*, which thickens the sound, giving it a fuller, more dynamic and spacious feel.

Pitch bend and modulation

With a *pitch bend* or *bender* you can literally bend the pitch up or down as you play. The *modulation* controller usually makes the sound vibrate. Quite often a single controller will operate both features.

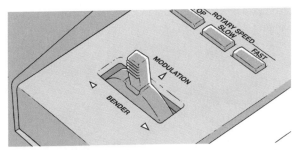

Moving this lever from left to right controls pitch bend; front to back movement controls modulation. (Roland)

Synthesizers

With *synthesizer* capabilities you're able to make sounds brighter or darker, longer or shorter, or even entirely alter their character.

Ribbons and beams

Alternative effect controllers are a ribbon, over which you slide your finger, or one or more infrared beams that allow you to control the effects simply by moving your hand towards and away from the light source.

CONNECTIONS

You can hook up all manner of gear to a keyboard or piano. Plug in headphones (to the *phones* socket) for silent practice, connect your instrument to a powerful amp for gigs (*output* or *line out*), use pedals, or even connect up your CD player (*input* or *line in*).

Rear panel of a keyboard, showing various inputs and outputs.

MIDI

If you have a home keyboard or a digital piano you can hook it up to another digital instrument, or even your computer. You do that with MIDI, which stands for *Musical Instrument Digital Interface*. Using special MIDI-leads/cables you can use your piano to play the sounds of a home keyboard, you can have your computer play the piano, have your computer record what you play, and do a great deal more. If you want to know more, then check out chapter 9.

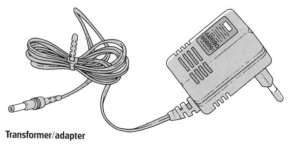

Transformer/adapter

Power

Most digital keyboard instruments operate at 9 or 12 volts DC. This low voltage is supplied by a transformer/adapter, which is generally internal or supplied as an outboard unit along with the instrument.

SEQUENCERS AND DISK DRIVES

Many, if not most, keyboards and pianos allow you to record your own playing on internal memory, and to save what you have played, using a built-in disk drive or other storage media. These drives can often be used for other purposes as well.

Sequencer

A *sequencer* is somewhat like a cassette recorder. You use it to record your playing, but instead of recording onto tape it stores your performance electronically, on a memory chip. Sequencers are also referred to as *recorders*.

A very basic sequencer which allows you to record four songs

Disk drive

Some sequencers only remember what you did until you turn off the power. Others will save what you recorded until they run out of memory. When this happens the only solution is to erase previous recordings to free up memory

Disk drive and floppy disk for saving your own work or loading songs and accompaniments

space. However, if your instrument has a built-in floppy or hard disk drive you can store everything you play indefinitely. Floppy disks can often be used to load new accompaniments, whole new songs, and – occasionally – new sounds as well.

3. LEARNING TO PLAY

So is it hard to learn to play keyboards? Yes and no, really. A keyboard has a nice simple layout which is easy to get to grips with. On the other hand, you need to get ten fingers to do exactly what you want them to, which can be pretty hard at first. The best answer is that it all depends on what you want to do. Besides, there is a considerable difference between playing the piano and playing the keyboard. Will you need to take lessons? Should you learn to read music? How much practice does it take?

If you want to play the basic melody of a song you just heard, it's easier to do so on a keyboard instrument than on a sax, or a violin. Why? Well, you can do it with just one finger, and the keyboard layout makes it pretty easy to find the right notes.

By ear

Many well-known musicians never had a lesson in their life; they learned to play by ear. You too can learn to play a keyboard instrument in this way.

The difference

Home keyboards are easier to learn without a teacher than pianos are. They do a lot of the work for you – chords, bass and drums can all be automated. All you have to do is play the melody, and again, just one finger will do. But if you want your investment to do a little more than that then you'll have to put in a little more effort, of course. In terms of learning to play, a digital piano is identical to an acoustic one.

15

READING MUSIC

Do you have to read music in order to play keyboard or piano? If you want to play classical music the short answer is yes. If you're going to be playing anything else, then the answer is no, not necessarily. Have you ever seen a keyboard player in a band reading sheet music? But then again…

Then again

… then again there's a very good case to be made for learning to read music. Consider the following:

- You'll have access to a vast amount of sheet music, including song books, books with cool (or hot) licks, transcriptions of your favourite players' solos, dexterity exercises and so on.
- If you can read music, you can write it too. That's handy when you've just created a tune and want to put it on paper, or write parts for the other band members.
- When you know how to read music, it'll be easier to grasp what other musicians are on about, and you'll know what they mean by crotchet/quarter note triplets or a diminished seventh chord.
- You may become a better musician when you can read music, rather than a simple keyboard player.
- Reading music isn't really that difficult. It just needs a bit of patience and application.
- And when the time comes, just forget about the notes again. You will play a lot better when you concentrate on the music instead of on the notes. And yes, that's exactly why all those keyboard players (not to mention concert pianists) don't use sheet music on stage.

TAKING LESSONS

When approaching a school or a teacher there are a lot of things you'll need to ask about. Here are a few pointers.

- Is an introductory lesson included? This is a good way to find out how well you get on with the teacher and, for that matter, with the instrument.
- Will you be required to practice at least three hours a day, or can you also join if you are just doing it for the fun of it?
- Is this teacher going to make you practice scales for two years, or will you be pushed onto a stage as soon as possible?

- What about instructional videos? Will you be able to borrow the tapes to study them at home?
- Do you need to buy lots of books, or is course material provided?
- Is it possible to record your lessons, so you can go over the material again at home?
- Is advice on purchasing instruments and other equipment included?

Group or individual tuition

You can take individual lessons or group tuition. Personal tuition is more expensive but can be tailored to your needs. Professional teachers will usually charge between £15–30/$20–50 an hour for individual lessons.

Home keyboard schools

Some manufacturers of home keyboards have their own teaching facilities where you learn how to play following their own methods on their keyboards.

Collectives

You can also check to see whether there are any teachers' collectives or music schools in your vicinity. These collectives may offer extras such as ensemble playing, masterclasses, clinics and other opportunities.

Cmin7

Chords can be written out note by note or be represented in shorthand by so-called *chord symbols*. In the latter case, you'll read abbreviations like Cmin7 or Asus9, instead of a stack of notes on a staff. Chord symbols are used in all sorts of music as well as in keyboard classes. Reading chords in the traditional way, therefore, is not always necessary. It's a different story, however, for the right-hand melody. This is usually written out – if you don't read music then learning it by heart is your only option.

Which keys?

Most instruction books have charts or diagrams showing which keys make up a particular chord. To find out which notes are implied by the chord symbols on your instrument's display or in instruction manuals, just ask your teacher or look them up in a book.

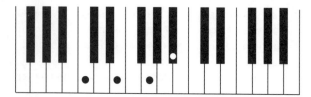

C dominant seventh chord (C7): C – E – G – B-flat

PRACTICE

Having an acoustic piano means the neighbours can always listen in. There are no such problems with a home keyboard or digital piano, which will probably suit you just as much as it will them. Just pop on some headphones or turn the volume down and you won't be overheard.

Digital or acoustic?

Even though digital pianos are getting to sound and feel more and more like acoustic ones, they're still not the same. So you may have to make adjustments if you want to practice on one and have your lessons on the other.

Half an hour

How much practice you need, again, depends on where you want to end. Many top players spent years practising for five or six hours a day or even longer. As with all other instruments the more time you put in the faster you'll progress, but half an hour a day is a good guideline if you want to make reasonable progress without spending too much time practising.

Books, videos, CDs, floppies

If you'd rather learn without a teacher then there's a lot of material out there for you to get your teeth into.

- Songbooks contain transcriptions of well-known songs, the best songs of a particular group, or a whole album in written form.
- Quite a few books come with a CD or cassette. These often include songs with the keyboard part deliberately left out, for you to fill in.
- Ordinary CDs and tapes are also great for playing along to. Many instruments have an input that can be used to connect a CD player, so that your playing and the sound of the CD will come out of the same speakers.

- Many instructional videos, often created and presented by well-known musicians, are available. With these you can take lessons from the masters, on screen.
- By now there are many inexpensive floppy disks containing full accompaniments to one or more tunes. Load it in and away you go.
- Keyboard magazines often publish useful playing tips, as well as transcriptions and exercises.

And finally ...

Two of the best ways to learn how to play are among the simplest. Play as much as you can, on your own or in a band. And go out to see other musicians play, too. Whether they are living legends or local amateurs, every gig you attend is an opportunity to learn something new.

4. BUYING AN INSTRUMENT

The very cheapest home keyboards cost less than £20/ $50, but they were not really designed for serious use. So how much should you spend, and what will that get you? This chapter covers prices, basic considerations and useful pre-shopping tips.

A decent entry-level keyboard will generally cost anything from £180/$300 upwards. The number of buttons, sounds and accompaniments on these instruments is usually pretty spectacular. So is there any sense in spending more?

Bigger, better
Yes, there is, since there's usually more than meets the eye to expensive instruments. First of all, they have more features, which you can read about in chapter 5. Second, they sound better. Chapter 6 deals with that subject. Finally, the accompaniment section, dealt with in chapter 7, may have more to offer.

Digital pianos
Digital pianos, on average, are more expensive than home keyboards. They usually have bigger and better keyboards, better amplifiers, more samples per sound, and wooden exteriors like real pianos. The outside doesn't always tell you where all the money has gone, however, so take a close look at chapters 5 and 6 first.

Acoustic pianos
What are the main differences between acoustic and digital pianos? The acoustic versions are more expensive than the

digital ones and they require more maintenance, including regular professional tuning, but they are 'real' pianos, with a piano's specific sound and touch, they can last at least a lifetime, and they retain most of their value if they're well looked after.

Home keyboard prices

It's not easy to split up the market, but here's a try. For between £180–550/$300–800 you will get a serious entry-level keyboard. An intermediate instrument with additional features such as built-in disk drives and better sounds might set you back up to £1000/$1500. Beyond this price range, at around £2000/$3000 and above, you'll find instruments that are mostly used by professional musicians.

Digital pianos

For a standard-level piano with 88 keys you might expect to pay anything from £900/$1200. More money often buys you an instrument with more features, sounds and power. Digital grands and top-of-the-range instruments with all the features you could dream of start around £3300/$5000. Professional stage pianos start at under £2000/$3000.

Getting better all the time

Drums, guitars and many other instruments can't really be improved a great deal. On the other hand electronic instruments, just like computers, get better all the time. Having bought the latest high-tech device, it won't be long before you find it's been replaced by a bigger, better and faster model costing the same or even less. There's not a lot you can do about this, and the pace of technological change is not likely to slow down in the near future.

Good idea

It's a good to have a rough idea of what you want before you go shopping. Some examples? If you only want a keyboard to help you work out some basic melodies then you don't need to spend more than £200/$300 at the most. If you want to take your instrument on the road then you will need to pay attention to things that are not important at all when you only play at home. A backlit display, readable in dim light, is one example. Some pianos have features more usually found on home keyboards, and some home keyboards have perfectly adequate piano sounds. So you will have to find out what the differences are, and exactly what it is that you yourself are looking for. This book will help you put those considerations into perspective.

Ask a friend

If you have a friend or relative who owns a home keyboard or a digital piano ask them if you can have a go on it. Experienced users know the pros and cons of their instrument, and they can also shed light on the usefulness (or uselessness) of certain features.

GOING SHOPPING

Spend some time shopping around. Don't just buy from the first shop that happens to stock what you want, unless you fall head over heels in love with a certain instrument – and even then it may be a good idea to stall. Listen to a variety of instruments, and listen to a variety of sales people as well; they have their own 'sound', too.

Make notes

It's hard to keep track of every detail of every instrument. So why not take notes when you're in the shop? Or you can do it the other way around; make a list of everything you want your instrument to do while you go through this book, and ask the sales staff which instruments fit the bill.

Demo demons

A demo option is a very common feature on digital instruments. Press the button and you will be treated to an impressive piece of music. Sales staff who restrict their input to hitting that button should generally be avoided. The least you should settle for is some information about what the instrument can do and a serious audition.

Just hit the demo button ... (right)

Part exchange

Want to trade in your current instrument? Then shop around, as some retailers offer better deals than others. But don't get your hopes up too high; as technology progresses and musical styles change by the day, home keyboards in particular tend to depreciate rapidly, losing up to eighty percent of their value within two or three years.

Cash and carry?

The sunny side? Electronic instruments are frequently sold at bargain prices to make room for the latest models, or for other reasons. They can look very tempting sometimes, but remember that good advice and service (after sales, too) can be invaluable where musical instruments are concerned.

SECONDHAND

There are plenty of used digital pianos and home keyboards out there at reasonable or even very attractive prices. Here are a few things to think about.

Your own styles

A 'vintage' home keyboard from 1993 won't have all the latest rave and hip-hop styles on board, simply because they didn't exist at the time it was built. Is this a problem? Not per se. Some of the more expensive keyboards allow you to program your own styles, or you might be able to buy new ones on disk.

Why (not) a dealer?

Secondhand instruments can be bought from dealers as well as from private individuals. Dealers take a cut, of course, so buying privately can often be cheaper. On the plus side, they usually offer better information, as well as a warranty, and you can often go back for service.

Where?

The best place to look for secondhand instruments apart from music shops is in the classified ads section of music magazines and newspapers, on the Internet, and on bulletin boards in stores and supermarkets. Alternatively, you could put in a wanted ad yourself. Details on music magazines are on page 122.

ANYTHING ELSE?

It's always a good idea to bring along an experienced keyboard player, maybe your teacher, when you go out keyboard-hunting, and particularly when buying second-hand. Two can see and hear more than one, even if you have learned this book by heart.

Catalogues, magazines and the Internet

Catalogues and brochures provide you with detailed information outlining the differences and similarities between a variety of models and brands. They're also designed to make you want to spend a lot more than you originally may have had in mind, so make sure you take a price list along. Magazines for keyboard players, as well as music magazines in general, often offer reviews of the latest instruments and plenty of additional information, as does the Internet. Addresses and URLs can be found on pages 122–123.

Fairs and conventions

One last tip: visit music trade fairs and music conventions if and when you can. Besides finding a considerable number of instruments to try out and compare, you will also meet plenty of product specialists as well as many fellow musicians, both of whom are good sources of information and inspiration. It is also useful to check out the demo sessions and clinics.

5. A GOOD ONE

They may all look pretty much the same, but they're not. Both home keyboards and digital pianos can differ widely in quality and capabilities. This chapter deals with most of the features that you can more or less judge without playing a single note: the keyboard itself, the controls, ease of use, various modes of display, pedals and more.

This and the three following chapters provide you with the basic information about sound quality (chapter 6), accompaniments (chapter 7), and connecting other equipment to your keyboard (chapter 8) that you need to go out and buy the best instrument you can.

THE KEYBOARD

The quality of the keyboard is a major factor in how pleasant an instrument is to play.

More, or less

Many digital pianos have 88-note keyboards – the same as most acoustic pianos. This corresponds to a range of seven octaves, an octave consisting of twelve black and white keys. Some pianos have 76 keys. This is not always done to cut costs, as some expensive instruments have fewer keys to make them easier to carry around.

Home keyboards

Many top-level home keyboards have 76 keys while others make do with 61 or less. If you're serious about keyboards, 61 is the absolute minimum. These instruments are often referred to as five-octave keyboards. A smaller one is only useful if you plan to use it to check out basic melodies.

88-, 61-, and 49-note keyboards.

Key width

The keys are usually the same width as normal piano keys: about 7/8" or slightly more than two centimetres. Narrower keys are not as easy to play.

Touch sensitivity

Most home keyboards and practically all digital pianos have *touch sensitive* keyboards; the harder you play the louder the sound. This feature is also referred to as *touch response* or *velocity*; rather than sensing how 'hard' you play, a touch sensitive key actually responds to the speed (velocity) at which you move it downward.

Not just louder

As you hit an acoustic piano key harder, the sound not only becomes louder, but a bit brighter, too. Guitars, violins and most other instruments respond in a similar way. High-quality keyboards and digital pianos are capable of reproducing those subtle changes.

Afterwards

Some instruments offer a second stage of touch sensitivity that kicks in once the key has been depressed: *aftertouch*. If you keep the key down and exert a little more pressure, you add a little extra colour or volume to the sound, or another layer, or some modulation, depending on the instrument and on your settings.

Letting go

An instrument with *release velocity* is also sensitive to the speed you let the keys go at. In practise this allows you to fade out strings gently as you bring up the keys, rather than chopping them off. These two features are found on top-of-the-range keyboards.

Playing style

On many pianos you can adapt the degree of sensitivity to your playing style. Set to *light* or *soft* you don't need a pianist's technique to produce loud notes. The *hard* or *heavy* setting will give you the widest dynamic range – from a whisper to a roar. In between the two the instrument will respond much as an acoustic piano does.

Harpsichords and organs

A number of keyboard instruments, such as the harpsichord and various types of organ, are not touch sensitive. If you want to truly reproduce the effect of instruments such as these, you need to able to turn off the touch sensitivity. In some cases this is done automatically when one of these sounds is selected.

Variations

The action of the keyboard may vary considerably from one make or series to the other: light or heavy, fast or sluggish, razor sharp or indifferent. What's best has as much to do with quality as with your preferences or your style of playing.

When trying out the feel and response of the keyboard, make sure that it's plugged in and producing a sound; nothing will feel good when it's silent.

Feel

To assess the actual quality of a keyboard, you can carefully move the keys sideways. There should be a little give at that point. All keys should feel the same and have the same, even response and action. No matter how hard you play, the keyboard should not rattle or buzz.

Softer

When you're using the built-in speakers you might not be able to get the lowest notes to sound as loudly and clearly as the high ones. With their limited dimensions (and often enough, a limited price) the speakers are not able to reproduce these low frequencies. If you hook the instrument up to an external keyboard amplifier (see chapter 6) the response is supposed to be even at all pitches, low to high.

Weighted keys

On an acoustic piano, the keys make felt-tipped hammers hit strings. The moving hammers give the instrument its characteristic playing action. Manufacturers of digital pianos try to match this action as closely as possible, usually by attaching a mechanism which mimics the feel of a hammered keyboard. This doesn't contribute anything to the sound; it just affects the way the keys feel. Keyboards with this sort of piano-like feel are known as *weighted, hammer action* or *hammered action* keyboards.

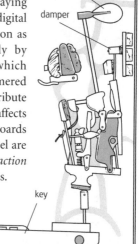

The hammer mechanism in an acoustic piano. The downward motion of the key makes the hammer hit the string, releasing the damper at the same time. When the key is released, the damper falls back into place, muting the string.

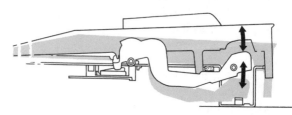

Weighted keyboard. The hammer, just beneath the key, serves to imitate the action of a real piano key.

TUNING

Unlike guitars or acoustic pianos, digital instruments don't need to be tuned note by note. The pitch of the entire instrument, however, can be changed in one of two ways.

Fine tuning

When you're playing in a band or playing along to a CD your instrument may sound a little *flat* (too low) or *sharp* (too high). Fine tuning or *master tuning*, usually controlled by a rotary knob or by up/down buttons, allows you to match your pitch exactly to the music.

Transposing

If, on an acoustic instrument, you want to play a song a number of notes higher or lower (i.e. *transposing* the song to another key), you'll have to use different keys, chords or fingerings. On a digital instrument transposing a song is a lot easier. You just raise or lower the pitch of the entire keyboard in semitone/halftone steps, and you'll produce the desired notes while using the same keys and chords that you're used to. Transposing is done with up/down buttons or, less commonly, a slider.

Transposing the instrument in halftones by means of a slider. In the position shown, pressing the C key sounds the note D.

One or two octaves

Instruments can often be transposed over a range of one or two octaves, sometimes even more. This feature also increases the range of your instrument; you can play higher and lower notes than the actual number of keys suggests. If the keyboard can be divided into two or more sections (*split*) then you can sometimes control the degree of transposition for each section. There's more about this on pages 41 and 42.

Scale tuning

The smallest available pitch interval on a keyboard instrument is the semitone/halftone: from one key to the next black or white key. In some styles however (Arabic and other Eastern musics, for example), *microtones* are used too. To play that type of music you either need an instrument with *scale tuning* or a so-called *Arabic scale converter* added to your instrument.

Historical and personal tunings
Over the centuries several different tunings (*temperaments*) have been used. In order for you to be able to play the music of specific eras with historical accuracy some digital pianos are able to reproduce these tunings. In addition, some pianos allow each key to be tuned individually, so you can have it tuned to your liking.

SELECTING SOUNDS
There are many different systems for selecting sounds and accompaniments on home keyboards. Pianos are simpler, so that's where this section starts.

Two at a time
Most pianos have one button for each available sound. Sounds can often be layered by simply pushing two buttons at a time, adding strings to the sound of an electric piano, for example.

Variations
Some pianos allow you to switch between two, three or more variations per sound; for example a basic piano might have rock piano, bright piano and honky-tonk piano as alternative colours or timbres. When using the layer feature, the variations are not always available.

Some pianos offer a number of variations on certain basic sounds.

More features
The more features a piano has, the more it will resemble a home keyboard in terms of looks and operation.

Keypad or display

The numerous sounds and accompaniment styles (perhaps hundreds of each) of home keyboards are usually selected by means of a numeric keypad, or by selecting options on the display. In both cases, you'll find that the available sounds and styles are divided into groups.

Groupings and banks

Sounds and accompaniments are commonly organized as groups of eight, the first group containing eight piano sounds, the fourth group guitars, the sixth group strings, and so on. If there are a great many sounds on board, you may come across other groupings. On some instruments, the available sounds are split into *banks*, with each bank further subdivided into smaller groups. A11, for instance, would then be a grand piano in bank A (of A and B), sub-group 1, sound 1. Accompaniments are usually grouped by style – pop, latin, jazz, dance, and so on, with each group containing a variety of patterns.

Calling up sounds

If the instrument uses a numeric keypad, the sounds and styles are usually listed on the front panel of the instrument. Selecting a sound or a style is a matter of punching in the number or code that corresponds to the option on the list – much as when dialling a phone number. The numeric keypad usually has a pair of buttons labelled *sound, tone* or *voice*, and *accompaniment, style*, or *rhythm*. Pressing these decides which the keypad entries affect.

PIANO	015 DULCIMER
000 GRAND PIANO	ORGAN
001 BRIGHT PIANO	016 DRAWBAR
002 E GRAND PIANO	017 PERC ORGAN
003 HONKY-TONK	018 ROCK ORGAN
004 ELEC PIANO 1	019 CHURCH ORGAN
004 ELEC PIANO 2	020 REED ORGAN
006 HARPSICHORD	021 ACCORDIAN
007 CLAVI	022 HARMONICA
CHROMATIC PERC	023 BANDONEON
008 CELESTA	GUITAR
009 GLOCKENSPIEL	024 NYLON STR GUITA
010 MUSICBOX	025 STEEL STR GUITA
011 VIBRAPHONE	026 JAZZ GUITAR
012 MARIMBA	027 CLEAN GUITAR
013 XYLOPHONE	028 MUTED GUITAR
014 TUBULAR BELLS	029 OVERDRIVEN GUI

Selecting sounds and accompaniments using a numeric keypad

Enter

Some instruments ask you to confirm a sound by pressing an enter button. This prevents you from making mistakes, but tends to slow things down.

Display

If there are more options to choose from than can be printed on the instrument, you usually have to go by the options shown on the display. You may have to use a button first to opt for a certain group of sounds. The guitar button, for instance, brings up a listing of all available guitar sounds on the display. You then pick the sound you want using a data entry wheel, cursor keys or soft keys, or the display itself if it's a touch screen.

Soft keys and alpha dials

Data entry wheel

Exactly what soft keys do changes with the information that's being displayed. A data entry wheel, also known as an *alpha dial, jog wheel, data entry dial* or just a *dial*, is a rotary control which controls a variety of things. If you've selected volume it acts as a volume control; when selecting sounds you use it to scroll through the list, and so on.

Buttons and cursor keys allow you to find the desired guitar sound

Variations

Like pianos, some home keyboards offer variations on each sound. One fine example is a grand piano sample, for instance, with variations representing the degree to which the lid is opened. And yes, some keyboards even show the corresponding lid angle on their display.

Wide open, completely closed, or anything inbetween...

Pads

Pads are finger triggers. Hitting them will activate drum sounds, sound effects, or, if they can be programmed, whatever else you want them to. Pads are also known as *touch pads*, or collectively as *touch keyboards*. They may or may not be touch sensitive.

High button count

Some keyboards have considerably more buttons than others, especially in the sound or style selection sections. One general remark: a high button count may look daunting, but it has its advantages. If the front panel is laid-out

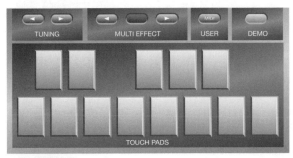

A touch keyboard

well and each function has a button, slider or dial to itself, life can be a lot easier in the long run. Easier, for instance, than having one button that you need to press seven times before you reach the option that you want. Remember, operations that at first seem quite inconvenient can eventually turn out to be extremely easy to work with, and vice versa.

PEDALS

Like acoustic pianos, digital pianos can't do without pedals, but pedals are often considered to be more of a luxury on a home keyboard.

On the right

The *sustain pedal,* operated with the right foot, allows the sound to ring on without you having to keep the keys down. Sustain pedal connections on instruments are marked *sustain, pedal* or *damper.* The last name refers to the fact that on acoustic pianos this pedal lifts all the felt dampers off of the strings.

On the left

The pedal on your left is the *soft pedal* or *piano pedal.* On an upright piano this pedal moves the hammers closer to the strings, reducing the volume and changing the tone.

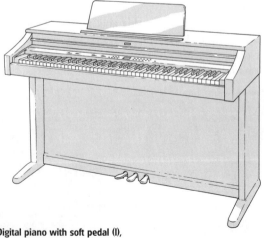

Digital piano with soft pedal (l),
sostenuto pedal (centre) and sustain pedal (r)

On a grand piano, it moves the whole action a little to one side, so that only one or two strings are struck instead of three. Hence the direction *una corda*, one string, used in written music to describe this effect. Digital pianos emulate this electronically.

In the middle
Some digital pianos have a third, middle pedal, known as the *sostenuto pedal*, Steinway pedal (after the famous piano makers), or Bach pedal (after the famous composer). Play a chord, then depress the pedal; the chord will be sustained, while any further notes you play won't.

Volume pedal
Organs were not originally touch sensitive; you use a *volume pedal* or *expression pedal* to affect the volume. You can also use such a pedal on a home keyboard.

Bass pedals
Separately available *bass pedals* with up to about thirty giant keys played with the feet to provide bass-lines are also a result of the home keyboard's organ ancestry. However, not every home keyboard can have bass pedals connected. Bass pedals are also known as *foot keyboards* or *pedal boards*.

Bass pedals

Single or multiswitch
Accompaniments can sometimes be operated by the feet as well, using either a single switch or a *multiswitch*, to start or stop the accompaniment, trigger variations and fills, and perform other tasks.

User-configurable pedals
Some pedals fill multiple roles; what they do depends on the socket you plug them into. There are also keyboards

with an *assignable jack* input (see page 72) which allows you to program what you'd like the appropriate pedal to do. For instance, switching effects on and off, acting as a sustain pedal or controlling the automatic accompaniment.

Quality

Like keyboards, pedals vary in price and quality. A basic sustain pedal can be had for £13/$20, but it won't be properly stage proof. Good pedals have a metal foot bar, a non-slip bottom and a rugged plastic or metal housing. They start at around £30/$40, and a decent volume pedal will set you back anything between £20–60/$40–100. Multiswitch prices depend on the number of switches involved, and they start at around £60/$75.

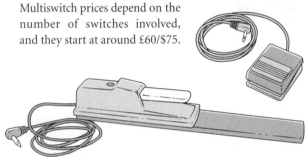

Pro- and entry-level sustain pedals

SEQUENCER

Most sequencers have controls similar to other recording devices such as cassette or mini disc recorders: play, stop, record, fast forward, and so on. Sequencers literally record the sequence of *events* that you perform.

Events

Simply playing one note can be broken down into a number of events; pressing the key and releasing it are two events, the velocity is a third event, and operating a pedal a fourth, to mention just a few examples. The amount of music a sequencer can record is usually expressed as the number of events it can hold in memory. A capacity of 30,000 to 45,000 events is not unusual for pianos. Because they need to contain accompaniments as well, home keyboards need larger memories. Top-level keyboards may go up to 250,000 events or more.

A lot more

Playing back your performances is a great way to judge your own playing, but sequencers have more to offer. You can play your left-hand part first, and play it back while practising the right-hand part. Or you can record a slow version and then replay it at a higher speed without the pitch being affected. This is invaluable when practising to get a tune up to tempo. Most keyboards also allow you to record entire songs and accompaniments with the on-board sequencer.

Common sequencer controls: record, rewind, start/stop, fast forward and pause. The illustration shows a three-track sequencer.

But not everything

Some sequencers only record when using the accompaniments. Others only work on chords, but not on melodies or solos. One more tip: as a sequencer records events, instead of sound, you can't include your voice in the recording.

Editing

Sophisticated sequencers allow you to edit your recordings. If you've played a bum note you'll be able to 'repair' the mistake, so you don't have to re-record the whole piece. Editing also enables you to transpose (see page 29) a sequence to suit a sax player or a guitarist, or to copy parts of one song to another, to add effects, to layer sounds, and a lot more.

Multitracking

Very basic sequencers have one single track. You play, it records: end of story. With two tracks you can often record your left hand on the first track, and then add your right hand on the second. Home keyboards often have eight tracks, but top-of-the-line models may have two, four or more times as many, allowing you to add parts to a song almost without limit.

Real time, step time

Most sequencers record in *real time*, which is similar to recording on a cassette deck or a mini disc. The alternative is recording in *step time*, which means entering the notes one at a time. Step time sequencing is rather like programming, and not much like playing. Most home keyboards will have both options.

Complicated

Check the manual if you intend to use your instrument for step time recording; there are wide variations in how easy these programming systems are to use. Some manufacturers simply have better systems than others. The same thing is true for the manuals themselves, by the way.

Resolution

Some sequencers record notes according to a grid. The finer this grid, the higher the *resolution*. The higher the resolution, the more accurately the sequencer will be able to reproduce the exact timing of the notes.

With a resolution of 48, there are 48 different points at which a note can be recorded within each beat (usually a crotchet/quarter note). But this isn't as accurate as it might sound, so if you would like to hear a true representation of your playing, you will need a resolution of 96 or 192 *ppq* (*pulses per quarter note*). Resolution is more properly called *quantize resolution*.

Limitless

Some sequencers can only handle one song at a time; recording a new song means that  you lose the previous one. Worse still, some cheap instruments erase the sequencer memory when you turn them off. You're better off with a sequencer that holds more than one song or *piece*, but if you really want limitless capacity, you need a disk drive.

EXPANDING YOUR INSTRUMENT

The 3.5" 1.44 megabyte floppy disk is still one of the commonest ways of storing and exchanging data, both for computers and musical instruments. Files for both tend to get bigger and bigger, requiring faster disks and more storage space, so that hard disks and other storage media are making their appearance.

Floppy disks

First, floppy disks. You can buy a disk of new accompaniments or a number of songs including lyrics and sheet music for about £5/$5 upwards. Floppy drives take a little time to access the information on disk, so it's preferable if your instrument allows you to move a whole batch of accompaniments from disk to memory at one fell swoop, since in this way you'll have instant access to them.

Direct access

Some instruments can read songs straight off the disk, bypassing the internal memory. The ten or twenty second gain this brings might not seem a lot, but when playing live it is a great help; even ten seconds is a long time to wait when you're on stage. Certain instruments allow you to keep playing while loading data from disk; this is known as *multitasking.*

Samples

Extra samples (so-called *WAV*-files) are available on floppy disk for those instruments that are able to read them. With the right equipment you can also record your own samples and load them into the instrument via floppy disk, or play them back by using MIDI (see chapter 9, page 73).

Standard MIDI files

There are two basic ways or *formats* in which an instrument can store a song on disk. One uses a proprietary format, which means that the file can only be read by instruments of that particular brand. The other is known as *Standard MIDI File format* (*MIDI File* for short), which can be read by any instrument that supports it. The down side is that MIDI files may take a little longer to save or load.

Hard disks

Built-in hard disks are faster and they can store a lot more information than floppies, but they're still quite rare. Connecting your instrument to a computer (using MIDI) allows you to use its hard disk, of course.

The Internet

Many companies will let you expand the sounds, styles or other features of your instrument via the Internet.

The march of time

Any storage medium that has been introduced for computer such as the 100 Megabyte ZIP disks or PCMCIA cards, finds its way to digital musical instruments as well, while 'older' and slower media (floppy disks, for example) are likely to become obsolescent.

PITCH BEND AND MODULATION

Two well-known effects that are found on practically any keyboard are pitch bend and modulation.

Pitch bend

Bending the pitch is exactly what a pitch bend does. It's a bit like the whammy bar (often called the *tremolo*, although it isn't really) on an electric guitar, and performs a similar function. You play one or more notes and bend them up or down to your liking. Some alternative names are *pitch*, *pitch shift*, *pitch bender* or *bender*.

Range

The degree of pitch bend is usually programmable. It's often set to bend up or down one whole tone, but it may be able to go up and down as much as an octave. Pitch bend controllers come in various guises. There are up/down buttons, levers or joysticks, trackballs and wheels, as well as alternative controls such as ribbons or infrared beams. Up/down buttons are less user-friendly than other controllers, which permit a more precise control of how fast the bend happens, and how far it extends in pitch.

Modulation

The most popular type of keyboard *modulation* is *vibrato*.

It's so popular, in fact, that one term often stands in for the other. Adding modulation makes the pitch wobble up and down quickly. Modulating a sound is done in the same way as pitch bending, and similar controls are used. In this case buttons don't allow fine control of the effect; they just turn it on or off.

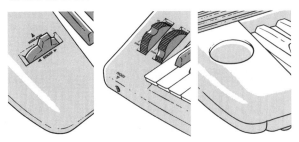

Lever (l), pitch and modulation wheels, trackball (r)

Simultaneously

Modulation and pitch bend can be used at the same time. A single integrated controller for both effects, such as a lever or a trackball, is neither better nor worse than two separate ones, like two wheels. It's more a matter of what suits you best. Accompaniments, by the way, don't respond to bending and modulation.

Effects

The sound shaping facilities of home keyboards and digital pianos don't end here. In addition to what's already been covered, there are built-in effects such as reverb and chorus, there are tone controls, and even the possibility to program your own sounds. There's more on this in chapter 6.

SPLIT

The *split* feature is used to divide the keyboard into two sections or zones, each with its own sounds or functions. On home keyboards, the left-hand section is mostly used for the accompaniment, and the right-hand section for the melody, but you can also play a double bass sound with your left hand, and a saxophone or other solo instrument line with your right. The inspiration for this feature may have been the twin keyboard of the organ, explaining why the zones are designated *lower* and *upper* respectively.

Floating and multiple splits

Most instruments have a *floating* or *programmable split*, so you can determine at what point the split occurs. Multiple splits are less common, but there are keyboards that you can divide up in a number of zones, each with its own sound. These zones can then be assigned their own pitch as well (transposing, see page 29), so you can, for example, alternate between a sax and a trumpet, playing them at identical pitches in different areas of the keyboard.

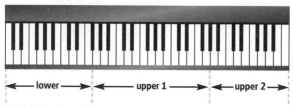

←— lower —→ ←— upper 1 —→ ←— upper 2 —→

Multiple floating splits

LAYER

The *layer* option, also known as *dual* or *dual voice*, allows two (and some-times more) sounds to be stacked on top of each other; when you hit a key, the sounds are blended together. The first sound in the stack on the

upper half of the keyboard is called *upper 1*, the next one *upper 2*, and so on. The lower half of the keyboard may have a layering option as well. The more layers you have available, the more flexibility you have in creating your own sounds.

Horn section

For instance, you could use four layers to make up your own horn section, either a traditional one, with a trumpet, an alto sax and two tenor saxes, or an alternative quartet of a soprano sax, a trombone and two tubas. Or you can use multiple layers to create a broad, fat-sounding string sec-tion by blending several string sounds at different pitches.

Combinations

Layers and splits can be used in a wide variety of combi-nations. Here's a very basic example. Use the lower part of the keyboard for one sound, the upper part for another, and add strings to both.

VOLUME

The *master* or *main volume* control determines the overall sound level. But there's also the matter of *balance*. The *accompaniment volume* or *balance* control sets the volume of the accompaniments in relation to the melody. The term *lower volume* refers to the volume level of the left half of the keyboard.

More volumes

Layers, splits and accompaniments bring a greater number of volume levels into play. Ideally, the volume of each part or section should be independently controllable, just as it would be in a recording studio.

This allows you to season organ sounds with just a pinch of strings, or serve strings with a large helping of organ, instead of hearing both voices at equal volumes. The more sophisticated (yes, and expensive) the instrument, the more independent volume controls will generally be available.

Accompaniment balance

On more sophisticated home keyboards you can also determine the balance within the accompaniments. A typical arrangement might have four controls marked *bass, drums, acc1* and *acc2 volume*. Acc1 and acc2 control two extra parts of the accompaniment, such as strings and horns (see chapter 7).

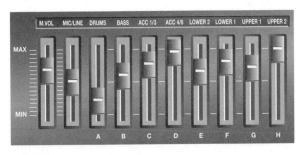

Separate controls for master volume, microphone level, drums, bass, accompaniments 1 to 3, and so on (GEM)

Dedicated controls

The simplest and fastest option is when each part or section has a separate volume control, as on a professional mixing desk; one glance tells you the exact settings. At the other extreme there are instruments on which you have to access the different volume settings via a function key, setting each value by using up/down buttons.

Faders

Sliding controls are known as *faders*. Fading in a sound is bringing it up, and fading it out is turning it down. Up/down buttons are not faders, even though they perform a similar function.

REGISTRATION MEMORIES

Ideally an instrument should be capable of memorizing all your settings, from sounds and effects to layers, splits, volume levels and everything else. *Registrations* or *registration memories*, as they are known, do this. They allow you to recall an entire set-up at the touch of a button, so you're ready for the next song in no time. *Performance groups* is one of the names used for groups that each contain several registration memories.

Registration memories (Yamaha)

DISPLAY

The display keeps you informed about what you (and the instrument) are doing. There are two basic display types: numeric and LCD.

Numeric

A *numeric display* is limited to showing numbers, and sometimes letters too. A numeric display might read T120, T standing for tempo and 120 being the number of beats per minute. SO34 would probably mean sound number 34. This type of display is common on cheaper home keyboards and on more expensive digital pianos; pianos don't have as many facilities, so there's little need for complex displays. In fact, some pianos don't have any at all.

A numeric display

LCD

LCD stands for *Liquid Crystal Display*. Pocket calculators and cell phones have this type of display too. All LCDs show you the selected sound, tempo and accompaniment, while the amount and type of additional information varies from one instrument to the next. The display may show balance and volume settings, or little icons (a tiny picture of a sax, say), telling you the type of sound you've selected. More recent developments are multitone or colour LCDs, and touch screens.

Contrast

The *contrast* control helps to improve the readability of the display under various lighting conditions. Not all instruments offer this control.

A display showing the accompaniment, the tempo, the effects and sounds that are being used, and more.

Backlit displays

LCDs can't be read in the dark, unless they are illuminated from behind. Fortunately, these *backlit* displays – cell phones have them too – are becoming increasingly popular. Some instruments have illuminated buttons as well.

Bigger

Home keyboards are making ever greater use of the display to select sounds, change settings, and so on. As a result, displays have steadily grown in size in order to offer as much information as possible at a glance.

Pages

Smaller displays need to use more pages, each of which holds a part of the information available. When you press the accompaniment button, for instance, the appropriate list of options automatically pops up on the screen.

The bottom of the pile

Inevitably, some pages will be at the bottom of the pile, which means having to go through all the other pages in order to reach them. User-friendly instruments offer faster ways to move through these digital piles than others – again, much like cell phones.

Monitoring

Some sophisticated instruments are capable of displaying the score of a song in real time as musical notation. Another

The score on display including lyrics and chord symbols

option is to display the lyrics, as you play; some instruments can display both simultaneously. Other displays show chord symbols, making it easier for other musicians to join in with you; they can read what you are playing rather than having to depend solely on their ears.

Multimedia
For such purposes it helps to have an instrument that can be connected to a TV or a computer monitor, so the singer or the other musician(s) don't need to breathe down your neck. Instruments with these capabilities are sometimes referred to as *multimedia keyboards*.

Educational displays
Some instruments tell you what keys are being pressed, either via the display or with little red or green lights (LEDs). This feature is sometimes used for teaching purposes, showing you exactly which keys you're supposed to hit next.

POLYPHONY AND MULTITIMBRAL
Early synthesizers were all *monophonic*: as with a sax or a trumpet, you could only produce a single (*mono*) note at a time. Nowadays all synths, as well as home keyboards and pianos, are *polyphonic*, so you can play chords on them (*poly* means many). Most are also *multitimbral*, meaning they can produce different sounds (*timbres*) at once.

Polyphony
Ten-voice polyphony is a minimum if you really want to play seriously, even on a piano, and even though you have no more than ten fingers. After all, if you sustain a chord and carry on playing you soon use more than ten sounds or voices simultaneously. For this reason, pianos usually have 32-voice polyphony, and as this is not enough for some types of music some even go up to 128. On home keyboards, a lot of the polyphony is used up by the accompaniments. Layering also takes its share; each note will use up as many voices as there are layers.

Multitimbral
A *16-part multitimbral* instrument is capable of having sixteen *different* sounds going on at the same time. This

may seem like a lot, but splits, layers, sustain and accompaniments may eat up these parts faster than you think.

THE MANUAL

Compared to the average piano home keyboards are complex instruments. A good manual is almost indispensable.

Mission impossible

Without consulting a well-written manual it's hard to discover all the options (especially some of the advanced or rarely used ones) that most home keyboards offer. The fact that controls often have multiple functions doesn't really help either.

Sweet clarity

Most manuals, though not all are reasonably well written and clearly laid out. The section on MIDI (see chapter 9) is usually the toughest, often requiring some prior knowledge. Check out the manual before you decide to buy an instrument; a good manual will tell you exactly what the instrument is all about.

COMPUTERS

Despite their appearance most electronic musical instruments are essentially computers that produce sound.

Operating System

Like computers, electronic instruments have *CPUs* (*Central Processing Units*) that handle all the internal data (sounds, effects, etc.). An electronic instrument will also have an operating system. Not Windows, nor DOS, System 9 or Linux, but something similar especially developed for the instrument. Some instruments can be upgraded by replacing the operating system with a newer version. These new versions can often be found on and downloaded from the Internet. If you are interested in learning more about computers with your keyboard, then check out chapter 9.

6. SOUND QUALITY

Keyboards and pianos are becoming more and more powerful and versatile, and the quality of the sounds is on the rise as well. What's the best sound? That really depends on the listener. But the more you yourself know about sounds, the more informed will be your choice.

Digital instruments use samples (digital recordings, stored on microchips) to generate sound. When it comes to the quality of these sounds there are two major factors. First, the number of samples to each sound, and second, the quality of the samples themselves. If you don't really want to go into this, then fast forward to page 51.

Three basic categories

The sounds on a typical home keyboard fall into three basic categories: samples of acoustic instruments, sound effects such as ringing phones and gunshots, and samples of synthesizer sounds. The latter are artificially made (*synthesized*) and may sound like anything from sci-fi soundtracks to bleeps, yelps and warbles.

The more the merrier

Imagine recording a saxophone on tape and then playing the tape back at double speed. Not only would the sax sound an octave higher, it would also sound different in character. It would also sound different to the same high note as played on the instrument itself. If you were then to double the tape speed again, the pitch would go up yet another octave. By that time it would be pretty hard to put a name to the original instrument. So for a sampled instrument to sound realistic at various pitches, it needs to have been sampled at various pitches.

One per octave

Many lower-cost keyboards use the one-sample-per-octave principle: with a five-octave keyboard, there is one sample for each octave of each sound, with five clavinet samples on board, five alto saxophone samples, and so on.

More per octave

More upmarket instruments will have a new sample every two, three or four keys. This makes the sampled instrument sound a lot more like the real thing.

One or more per key

Good digital pianos have more than one sample per sound per key. After all, most instruments not only sound louder when they're played harder; they also sound brighter. To reproduce these changes faithfully digital instruments use several samples made at various volume levels for each note.

Sample your own

You can make your own samples if you have either a dedicated sampler (see chapter 12), an instrument with a built-in sampler, or a computer with a soundcard, the appropriate software and a microphone, recording straight onto the hard disk. The files that you create that way are so-called WAV-files, 'WAV' being the extension of the file-name (i.e. PIANO.WAV). More and more keyboards are

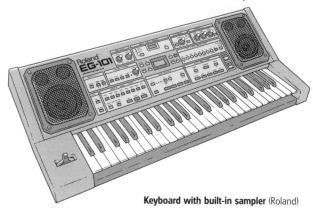

Keyboard with built-in sampler (Roland)

able to read these files, allowing you to add both commercially available and home-brewed samples to your sound library.

Good samples

Samples come in various formats and if you want to follow that up, you're bound to come across specifications of bits and kilohertz. For this book it suffices to say that more is better. An example, nevertheless? Good-quality samples are made in the same format as standard audio CDs, i.e. 16-bit at 44.1 kHz. Anything in excess of that brings about a potential increase in sound quality. The greater the number of bits, the better the sample will be able to convey dynamic variations (soft to loud), and the lower the level of background hiss. The higher the number of kilohertz the more extended the high-frequency response will be, resulting in a brighter, richer sound.

THE SOUNDS

Ultimately, instruments should be judged by the sound they make. In judging digital keyboard instruments, it's best to start by listening to the sounds you're likely to use most. On a home keyboard this will usually be one or two pianos and organs, as well as strings and brass instruments. Excellent handclap and seashore samples may be impressive, but are rarely of much musical use.

One at a time

When comparing keyboard instruments do this one type of sound at a time. Select the best piano sound on each instrument and then compare them. Do the same with the organs, the strings, and so on.

Don't forget to check out the bass and the drum set (drums and cymbals), as these instruments play an important role in your digital band.

The same day

Sound is not an easy thing to remember, so comparing instruments is best done in one session and in a single shop. Remember, however, that your ears are bound to need a break before you think they do. So take five, now and then. It works.

Whiz

If you want to get to know an instrument's sound library it's easiest to whiz through all the sounds using the up/down buttons or a similar control. The same thing goes for the accompaniments.

The range

Try the main sounds throughout their range. Most sounds do very well in the middle of the keyboard, but do they still sound as realistic in the high and low registers? On lower-quality instruments, some samples only sound good within a very small range.

The natural range

Do remember, however, that 'real' instruments do have limited ranges. You can't expect an alto saxophone sample to sound like an alto saxophone when played below or above its natural range, or a choir to sound like anything produced by a human throat when played at the extreme ends of the keyboard.

Tips

- When comparing instruments and sounds make sure you set the volume to equal levels. Some home keyboards may have relatively loud organs, others loud strings and so on.
- Organs, synth sounds, flutes and drum sounds are relatively easy to sample, so they will usually sound good. Pianos, guitars, saxes and cymbals are a lot harder to get right.
- String sections often sound better than individual string instruments like the violin and the cello.

Headphones

Decent quality headphones (starting at around £50/$80) usually produce a better sound quality than the built-in speakers. If you intend to use external amplification, auditioning the instrument via phones will give you a more honest impression of how good the sounds really are. Headphones are also effective in comparing similar sounds on various instruments; if you listen without headphones, then you're also comparing the speakers of the instruments.

The difference

One major difference between acoustic and electronic instruments is that acoustic instruments are endlessly expressive. Take a saxophone. Have someone play it. Have someone else play it. Get them to play it louder, or change their air stream. Change the mouthpiece. Change the reed. And every time the same sax will produce an entirely different sound. Digital instruments don't respond that way; they're less expressive, no matter how many features they have. They do, however, offer possibilities that acoustic players can only dream of.

The message

In the end, the quality and usability of the sounds of a digital musical instrument are more important than the number of sounds, effects or gadgets that you're offered. But on the other hand the larger the number of sounds, effects and other tweaks available to you, the better chance you've got of ending up with a few really excellent ones.

EFFECTS AND SYNTHS

Reverb and chorus are effects that you'll find on almost every keyboard and piano (see page 11). Some instruments go far beyond those two, with features ranging from programmable multi-effects to elaborate tone controls or synthesizer sections.

DSP

Digital instruments come with digital effects, generated and controlled by a *Digital Signal Processor* (*DSP*). Instruments may have more than one DSP, allowing several effects to be used at once.

Delay, phasing and flanging

Effects don't change the sound fundamentally, but add to it. *Reverb* is the most obvious example, adding warmth to sounds which would sound too 'dry' without it. Another popular effect is *delay* or echo. A very short delay effectively thickens the sound, while long delay  times allow you to play along with the echoed notes.

Phasing adds a swirling effect, and *flanging* creates a sound that has been likened to a jet plane passing overhead.

Tweaked to your liking

More sophisticated instruments may offer a number of variations on every major effect type, and can often be tweaked to your liking. Delay effects may have adjustable delay times, so you can set the time lapse between the original sound and the echo. Wavy effects such as chorus and phasing may be adjusted in terms of the depth and speed of the waves, and flangers may allow you to toy around with the distance between the sound and the 'jet plane', reducing it to a slight metallic edge. The more parameters you can adjust and the more precisely you can adjust them, the more musical use the effect will generally have.

Harmony

Harmony, also known as *harmonizing* or *pitch shifting*, adds an extra pitch to the note being played; it makes it sound as if you were playing two keys instead of one. You can set the interval (the 'musical distance') for this extra pitch, and intelligent instruments take the chords and the melody into account as well, preventing off-key notes from coming into play. Some instruments are able to add two new pitches to an existing one, allowing you to play chords with a single finger of either hand.

Arpeggio

Another way of creating the impression that you are doing more than you really are is to use an *arpeggio* or *arpeggiator*. You play a chord and the arpeggiator makes it sound as though you're playing its notes in rapid sequence, repeating and at impressive speed.

Panning

Using *panorama* (*pan*, for short) you can position an instrument in the stereo mix anywhere from far left to far right.

Leslie

Leslie cabinets were made popular by Hammond organ players. The Leslie sound is created by a rotating horn and a rotating drum which make up part of the speaker, literally swirling the sound around. Since Leslie is a registered trademark, digital simulations of this effect are given such names such as *rotor*, *rotary* or *spatial sound*.

Tone controls

Another popular sound-shaping device is the *equalizer*, which allows you to cut (decrease) or boost (increase) certain frequency ranges – just like the treble and bass controls on a hi-fi amp. The most basic equalization, found on some lower-priced pianos, is a switch with the options mellow, normal and bright. Slightly more sophisticated is a *brilliance* control with up/down buttons. A tone control with separate controls for a number of different frequency ranges is known as a *graphic equalizer*, and is mostly found on more expensive digital pianos.

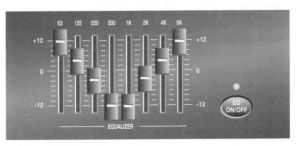

A graphic equalizer

Synthesizer

Home keyboards sometimes have synthesis options on board. These are usually simplified versions of systems found on real synthesizers, allowing you to give sounds smoother or sharper attacks, rounder or more angular 'shapes', brighter swells, or you can make them change their timbre through time or play them backwards. A synth option allows you to reshape the available sounds from the ground up.

ADSR

The *ADSR* section of a synth addresses the four sound parameters: attack, decay, sustain and release. The *attack* part of a sound is the time it takes to reach its maximum. The *decay* is the rate at which the volume decreases from that maximum. The *sustain* is the level of the sound while the keys remain pressed. The *release*, finally, governs the duration of the sound after the key has been released.

Envelope

A piano sound, for example, has a sharp attack, created by a hammer hitting a string. The attack is very brief, but the sustained note dies out slowly. An ADSR allows you to reverse those elements. You can have the tone gradually come up in volume, starting at zero, and make it sound for as long as you like after releasing the key, all very much unlike the real thing.

Trying the extremes is a good way to get familiar with what these devices can do – yet most musicians find the original settings more practical. ADSRs are also known as *envelope generators* or *envelopes*.

Memories

Instruments with these types of sound-editing options usually have memories in which to store the changes you've made to the sound.

AMPLIFICATION

What a keyboard instrument sounds like has, of course, a lot to do with the quality of its built-in amplifier and speakers. However large and heavy the instrument may be, it is safe to say that you can get a better sound by using external amplification – which can easily weigh and cost twice as much as the instrument itself.

Good enough

As long as you play at low volumes the internal amplification may be all you need. Turning the volume up will often cause the sound to distort, resembling that of an overdriven guitar.

Distortion usually sets in at the lower frequencies first. Only top-level instruments can be expected to sound good at high-volume levels.

What's watt?

The typical power output of home keyboards and digital pianos is usually somewhere between 5 and 12 watts. That's plenty for home use. More expensive pianos have more powerful amps, with maybe 30, 40 or more watts per channel to handle the wider dynamic range these instruments have.

Speakers

When it comes to speakers size isn't everything. There are good small ones and less good large ones. Most instruments have two speakers (stereo: one left, one right). More advanced models have four or more, which also helps to approximate the spatial characteristics of acoustic instruments such as the piano.

Hi-fi

The best way to judge speakers is to listen to them much as you would a pair of hi-fi speakers. How's the balance between low end, midrange and treble? Can they handle strong bass sounds and electric guitar stabs without distorting? How realistic does the piano sound? A tip: hit the demo button and listen from a distance. That's where your audience will be, after all.

Samples

Many brands use the same quality samples for instruments in various price ranges. In such cases the more expensive ones simply sound better because they have better amplification.

Home sound systems

An easy way to make your instrument sound better is to hook it up to a good home sound system, provided that it's capable of handling a keyboard instrument. Take care to read the appropriate manuals and pages 70–72 of this Tipbook in order not to damage any of the equipment involved.

Combo amps

If you need more power and portability, you're in for a pair of combo amps. A combo keyboard amp is a single cabinet with an amp and usually two speakers; a bigger one (usually 10", 12" or 15") for the low- and mid-range frequencies and a horn (tweeter) for the highest frequencies. Always go for dedicated keyboard combos, and don't use guitar or bass amps.

More watts

You can expect decent results from combo amps rated at 60 watts or above. These generally start at around £250/$300. Cheaper ones may not be as effective, though they will still outperform the internal amp and speakers. When looking at the prices of combo amps, be aware that you will probably need to buy two of them as a single amp will not give you the stereo sound a keyboard is capable of. Stereo will enhance most effects, and it'll make the overall sound come to life.

Combo amp (mono)

Performing

For live performances in modest venues, you need more power. Go for at least 100 watts and be prepared for a good one to set you back some £500/$700 or more – that's £1000/$1400 for the pair.

Watt, again?

When checking out amps, be aware that there are two different sorts of watt. If musicians (or books) talk about a 100-watt amplifier, they are referring to the volume (expressed in watts RMS) that the amp produces. The 100-watt (RMS) amp in this example may easily have a power consumption of 350 watts.

Other musicians, too

Keyboard amplifiers are designed to reproduce sounds in a very natural way without adding too much colour to them – unlike guitar amps, for instance. This is what makes keyboard amps also suitable for amplifying singers, wind players and other acoustic musicians. For that purpose they usually come with a few extra inputs, a dedicated microphone input and some basic mixing facilities, allowing them to be used as a miniature sound system. Of course any digital instrument can be hooked up directly to a professional sound system (PA), too.

Makers
Well-known manufacturers of keyboard amps include Carlsbro, Fender, Peavey, Roland and Yamaha.

Stage pianos
Stage pianos don't usually have any amplification built in. If they do, it will be in the shape of a low-powered practice amp. Headphone outputs are always provided, of course.

7. ACCOMPANIMENTS

Two home keyboards, each set to the same style of accompaniment, can sound totally different to one another; not just in terms of the patterns and sounds themselves, but also because auto-accompaniment sections differ widely in terms of features and options.

Automatic accompaniers go by lots of different names, including *style, arranger, rhythm* and *conductor*. 'Rhythm' is a bit of a misnomer, as there is a lot more to accompaniments than rhythm alone. The word 'style' is also often used to describe the various accompaniment patterns. An instrument with a hundred styles has a hundred different basic patterns.

Sensible styles
Every brand or series of keyboard has its own version of a certain number of styles. When comparing instruments, pay particular attention to the styles you're most likely to use, but don't forget to check out the ones you're unfamiliar with. They may inspire you to play things you've never even dreamt of.

Comparing styles
When comparing instruments set them to the styles that are relevant to you, and decide which you prefer. There's not much point in going through all the styles on one instrument first, and then repeating this process with the next.

Busy or relaxed
When you're making your choice, it may be helpful to try

to define what you hear. Some manufacturers go in for very busy accompaniments, with a lot of drums and percussion, busy bass lines and stacks of chords, while others consistently prefer more sparse arrangements. Most of the time, however, it's somewhere in between – a bit busier for a jazz style than for a slow ballad, for example. The number of 'players' in an accompaniment can sometimes be controlled. In a basic form, you can switch between *small* and *large* ensembles. More advanced systems allow you to switch individual 'players' on or off, or change their volume levels.

New bass player, new drum set

Take some time to judge the accompaniments. Once you've made your choice, your 'digital bass player' is there to stay, and the same goes for the rest of the band. Unless, that is, your instrument allows you to adapt the accompaniments, or create your own from scratch. There's more on this later. The more sophisticated instruments may allow you to change the drum set being used, for example.

Bare accompaniments

A tip: start off by listening to only the bare accompaniments, without playing any chords. Then when you do hit a chord, you'll be able to tell how everything fits in together. Busy, flashy accompaniments may sound impressive, but they can become annoying if they leave hardly any room to play anything yourself.

One by one

If you want to get the full picture then use the up/down buttons to zap through the accompaniments one by one. The number of variations on a style is important, especially if the instrument doesn't let you create your own. Hearing the same band play the same country groove in every country song soon becomes a drag both for you and your audience.

Groove control

Speaking of grooves: some keyboards allow for *groove control*, slightly altering the exact timing of the notes being generated and creating a different rhythmic feel.

One touch

Quite a few home keyboards are able to match suitable sounds to the chosen accompaniments automatically. *One touch* is one of the names given to this feature. A single key press, and the instrument automatically picks a heavily distorted guitar to play the lead in a rock song, or a late night sax for the solo in a bossa nova. Suitable effects and layers may be chosen automatically as well.

Volume

Some accompaniments are capable of responding to the volume level that you are playing at. When you play softly, the band follows – just like a real ensemble would, or at least should – and vice versa.

Orchestration

Sophisticated accompaniments can be made to sound even more lifelike by dividing them up into a number of *orchestras*. The piano part could make up the first orchestra, with the strings providing the second orchestra with a different melody, and the brass playing the parts in a third one.

STYLES

There are two basic types of accompaniment: the traditional type, ranging from foxtrots to country, swing and pop, and the contemporary type, including styles such as techno, jungle or drum'n'bass, not to mention the styles that'll be launched next week. As new music styles go in and out of fashion faster than hemlines, it's hard for any home keyboard to be fully up-to-date. If an instrument can be fed new accompaniments (on floppy disks, or any other way: see page 39) it's much less likely to go out of style; instruments with programmable accompaniments can also be kept up-to-date (see page 69).

Tempo

Accompaniments usually sound best within a certain tempo range. Tangos don't sound good at thrash metal speeds, which is why every accompaniment has a start-up tempo assigned to it. This tempo may be recalled when the accompaniment is selected, or you may need to simultaneously press the up and down buttons, for example, in order to call it up.

Up and down

The tempo is shown on the display as the number of *beats per minute* (*BPM*). A tempo of 120 BPM has two beats per second: this is a popular tempo for marching music and for many types of dance music. It pays to experiment with the assigned tempos, as some accompaniments may sound great at unconventional speeds.

THE BAND

Most accompaniments have a drummer and a bassist as a basic rhythm section, the chords being provided by harmony instruments such as a guitar or a piano, with added strings, woodwinds, brass or other melody instruments and some percussion to spice things up. But how does this all actually work?

Tracks

Accompaniments have several *tracks*, with each track dedicated to one or more 'members' of the band. Having eight tracks is like having eight cassette decks, each one playing a tape containing the part of one or more band members.

The foundation

Often there is a track each for the drummer and the bass player, who lay down a foundation for the other musicians to build on. Drummers in particular can radically influence the sound and feel of a group, so make sure you like your drummer and the drum sound. Bass sounds vary from style to style. Some use an upright bass or acoustic bass, as it's also known, others use an electric bass guitar or a synthesized bass sound.

Acc1, acc2, acc3

The remaining tracks are dedicated to harmony and any additional instruments. If you can adjust the volume or other settings per track, you'll find that they are marked *acc1*, *acc2*, *acc3*, and so on, *acc* of course being short for accompaniment.

Three to eight

The number of available tracks varies from instrument to instrument. More sophisticated keyboards have eight, and some top-of-the-range models have thirty-two or even more tracks. Should you want to program your own accompaniments and have a feel for complex arrangements or lots of different things going on at the same time, you'll want as many tracks as you can afford.

CHORDS

Playing chords on a piano means exactly that: using your fingers to press each key necessary to form the chord. Home keyboards allow you to play chords with only one finger. Here's an introduction to the various automatic chord systems and how to use them, and for starters, the world's most basic explanation of what chords actually are.

Three or more

A chord is three or more pitches sounding simultaneously. Chords each have a specific character. Here are the simplest examples. A C major chord is made up of the notes C, E and G. The appropriate chord symbol is simply the letter C.

Minors and dominants

Changing the E to an E-flat (the black note to the left of the E) changes the chord to a C minor (C – E-flat – G, indicated as Cm), which sounds totally different. Sadder, most people say. Adding a B-flat to the C major chord produces a C dominant seventh (C – E – G – B-flat: C7), with a different character again.

One finger

On a home keyboard you can play chords with just one finger. Simply switch to the setting called *one finger chords*, *single finger chords* or *intelligent chords*, and playing a C on the bass end of the keyboard will (usually) produce a C major chord.

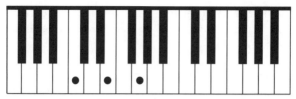

C major or C (C – E – G)

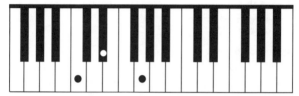

C minor or C m (C – E-flat – G)

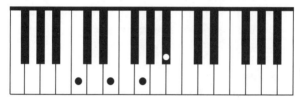

C dominant seventh or C7 (C – E – G – B-flat)

Keys become buttons

With the above setting, a C minor chord might be produced by playing both the C and D keys, and a C7 would require adding another note to that: the E, for instance. Creating chords in this way, is more like operating switches than playing keys, as it were: pressing three adjacent 'switches' adds up to a C7.

Fingered

Setting the keyboard to an option with a name like *fingered* or *fingered chords* allows you to play chords in the usual way, as you would on a piano. For this, you'd still be using the bass end of the keyboard, triggering the accompaniment as you go.

Calling all keys

A third setting (*piano style*, *whole key*, *full keyboard* or *full*) senses the entire keyboard, deducing the chord – and thus driving the band – from whichever three notes are being played at that time. This takes some getting used to; as most three-note combinations make up a chord of some sort, you may at first send the band places you never intended it to go.

Normal

Finally, there's a fourth setting (usually called *normal*) that turns off the accompaniment section. You may be able to keep a rhythmic backing going yourself, but the rest of the band won't be around.

Real bass players

If you're a bass player and you want to take it easy, you only play the so-called *root note* of each chord that passes by. The root note of any C-chord is C. Most bass players do at least a little more than that, for example by playing any of the other notes that make up the chord. Features with names like *bass inversion* or *revolving bass* are capable of imitating this sort of variation.

Inversions

There are plenty of other systems which can add life to accompaniments. Some instruments, for instance, are able to play the same chord in a number of different ways, just as keyboard players do when playing the chords in the traditional fashion. This type of variation, known as *chord inversion*, is simply a matter of changing the order of the notes in the chord. For example, from, C – E – G to G – C – E. It's the same chord, but it has a slightly different sound. Some keyboards even have accompaniments that respond to inversions that you play yourself.

The entire song

Want to sit in and play some solo over a band that runs down the entire song, including the chord changes, bass lines and rhythm? Some keyboards offer *jam tracks* or *free sessions* especially for this purpose. The instrument plays, you follow.

G seven flat-nine flat-thirteen

Chord options don't end at the three types mentioned so far. There are dozens of them, and each one can be built on any note on the keyboard. What about a G seven flat-nine flat-thirteen (G, B, F, A-flat, E-flat, often written as G7-9-13), for example. Not all accompaniments can deal with exotic chords like that, but you can always play them yourself, of course.

Limitations

As most players improve they start to play chords in the traditional way, like piano players do. You're more versatile that way, as even the most advanced automated chord systems have their limitations. You may need to be a quite advanced player to really explore that side of things, however.

VARIATIONS AND FILLS

Accompaniments, like songs, consist of various sections linked to one another in sequence. They might start off with an intro section, go on to a basic pattern, add a fill, return to a variation on the basic pattern, and then finish off with an ending. Selecting the various sections is done by means of a series of buttons, a pedal, or a multiswitch, and you may find some additional functions as well in this area.

Start and stop

Usually there's a single button which starts and stops the accompaniment. Pressing start will activate the drummer, maybe a percussionist too. The other band members keep quiet until you tell them which chord to play.

Intro and ending

An *intro* is the section that starts off the song. Pressing the *ending* button brings the song you're playing to a close. As an alternative, you can use *fade out* to gradually reduce the sound to silence.

Accompaniment controls (GEM)

Variation

Every basic accompaniment pattern has at least one variation. If you're using the basic pattern for the verses of a song, you simply hit *variation* when you come to the first chorus section. This usually spices up the arrangement a little. You return to the basic pattern by hitting a button marked *standard* or *original*. (There may be more than one variation to each accompaniment.)

Fill-ins and breaks

A *fill-in* or *fill*, often used to link two sections in a song, is usually one or two bars of drums. Some accompaniments offer a choice of fills. A *break* is when the accompaniment briefly stops, leaving a gap for the lead singer or instrumentalist to fill before the accompaniment kicks back in again on the next bar. On a home keyboard, fills and breaks are cued by hitting the appropriate buttons.

Synchro start

When using *synchro start*, the band won't kick in until you play a chord. This allows you to play an intro melody with your right hand, dropping the accompaniment in later with your left. *Synchro stop* ends the accompaniment the moment you release the keys.

Hold

The *hold* option, permanently switched in on most instruments, does the opposite: it ensures the accompaniments keep running regardless of whether you are playing or not. Switching off hold, if the instrument has that option, will stop the chord and bass parts of the accompaniment as soon as you release the keys. Only the drums will be left playing.

Mix 'n' match

Fully featured auto-accompaniments allow you to mix and match all kinds of options: fills with variations, synchro starts with intros, and so on.

Tap tempo

The tempo of a song can sometimes be set by simply tapping it in on a button. Just hit the *tap tempo* a couple of times in the desired tempo, and the orchestra will pick it up.

Display tempo, bar and beat

An instrument will usually let you see the tempo as well as hear it, with an LED flashing in time with the music. Larger displays often tell you the bar number (i.e. how many bars or measures you've already played), and on which beat of that bar you are.

DO-IT-YOURSELF

More sophisticated instruments allow you to sequence your own songs and accompaniments, or adapt existing accompaniments by changing bass patterns, adding a little piano, subtracting a bit of percussion, or whatever you fancy.

Modern times

Modern programming options allow you to customize the instrument not only to your personal taste, but also to follow the latest musical trends. Programming a full accompaniment is no mean feat however: every part and every section has to be composed and programmed into the sequencer.

Quantizing

It's not easy to play perfectly in time, and this is especially noticeable when recording. A so-called *quantizing* option, available on many instruments, corrects your timing errors and makes your playing sound really tight. It's most useful for laying down drum and bass parts.

Storage

Instruments that have the option to program or adapt accompaniments always enable you to store what you did, either in memory or on disk.

8. CONNECTIONS

Headphones, amplifiers, speakers, mixers, you name it; most keyboards and pianos come with a host of inputs and outputs for a host of possibilities. Pedal connections have been fully covered in chapter 5, but there are many more. There's also MIDI, a subject important enough for it to have the whole of chapter 9 dedicated to it. This chapter deals with the remaining connections.

Before you connect any cables to your instrument or any other electric or electronic devices, always read the relevant manuals. One more warning: always turn all relevant volume controls right down when connecting or disconnecting musical instruments, amplifiers and other devices.

Phones

The most familiar output is marked *phones*. Having two of these headphone outputs is useful, especially for lessons. It can double as an output to a home stereo system, for example, which can then be used for amplification or recording. If you do this, remember that the headphone output produces a pretty strong signal. Set the volume control on your instrument no higher than a quarter of the way to full, and then use the amplifier's volume control as the master control. This will usually prevent overload and possible damage to the amp and speakers. Turn down all volume controls as soon as the sound shows any signs of distortion.

A dedicated audio output is better suited to the task of driving an external amplifier, so if your instrument has one, use it.

Audio out

The audio output, labelled *line out, audio out* or just *output*, is the best one to use to connect your instrument to an external amplifier. Audio out is usually in stereo, using two sockets/connectors: one for the right, and one for the left channel. One of these sockets will be labelled mono. If you have a mono keyboard amp, for example, then you would use this socket.

You can't be too careful

Even standard audio outputs are pretty powerful, so again be careful when connecting your instrument up to your home stereo. Cranking up the volume on either instrument or the amplifier can easily cause damage.

Noise

Always adjust the volume levels of the instrument and the external amp for minimum noise (hiss) levels. If your instrument's volume control is set too low, the amp has to put in extra work to provide the desired sound level, resulting in hiss. The instrument itself can also be a source of noise; cheaper instruments tend to be worse in this respect. If your instrument's volume control is set too high, the sound may distort.

Never

Never (never ever!) connect your keyboard instrument to the *phono* or *disc input* of your home sound system, as this input is designed to handle only the very weak signals from a record player. Use the line, tape, CD, aux or tuner inputs instead.

Speakers off

When using external amplification, you may still hear the instrument's own speakers. If you can't turn them off, or turn them down without reducing the overall output to zero, then plug your headphones in. This switches the speakers off, but a little sound will still leak through the headphones themselves.

If you want something even quieter then you can use a stereo headphone adapter, available at electronics stores. Some instruments have separate volume controls for speakers and audio outs.

Audio in

The audio input (or *line in*) of your instrument can be used to connect other electronic instruments or an external sound module to your instrument's amp and speakers. Another option, which is extremely handy for practising, is to connect a CD-player or a cassette deck with play-along material. If you want to connect a mono source, make sure you connect it to the input on your instrument labelled 'mono'.

Assignable jack

The *assignable jack* input is intended for a pedal. This pedal can have one of several functions assigned to it, using the instrument's panel controls. Depending on the keyboard's capabilities, it may be used to start and stop accompaniments, select rhythms, provide sustain, and so on.

Microphones

A dedicated microphone input allows you to add a voice or an acoustic instrument to the mix. Used in this way, your home keyboard becomes a miniature sound system, sometimes including possibilities such as adding a little (indispensable) reverb to the vocal sound. The microphone input will usually have its own level control.

Computers

Connecting keyboards and pianos to computers is the subject of the next chapter.

9. MIDI

MIDI, a system with practically infinite options and power is a subject important enough to merit an entire chapter to itself.
MIDI is an interface which allows musical instruments, computers and a host of other digital devices to communicate with each other, and although a full treatment would deserve an entire book, the basics here will get you started.

MIDI allows you to control the sounds of a synthesizer by playing the keyboard of your digital piano. Or you can hook up a bass module to your home keyboard, adding a variety of bass sounds to your collection. And when you connect your keyboard instrument to a computer, the latter can become anything from an infinitely patient teacher to a recording studio.

Interface
MIDI stands for *Musical Instrument Digital Interface*. MIDI enables electronic keyboards, computers, sequencers and other devices to exchange all kinds of data with each other. Notes. Effects. Volume levels. Duration. Almost anything. MIDI can also be used to record or to exchange files (Standard MIDI Files), among other possibilities.

Telephones
So MIDI is about communication. Just like a telephone network, in fact. And just as any brand of phone can be used to ring any other, MIDI works regardless of the instrument's type or make.

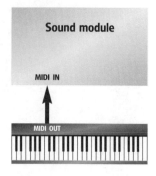

It might be a piano controlling a synthesizer module, or a home keyboard controlling a piano module. MIDI allows endless possibilities.

How it works

With MIDI you can't see what's going on. So how does it work? It's not really as complicated as it's usually presented. Here's a comparison. If you print out a letter that you wrote on a computer, the computer sends the letter to the printer as a series of codes. The printer then turns these codes into characters on the printed page. You can't see what happens, and you don't need to understand how it happens, but it does happen. You get your print-out.

The same lines

MIDI works along the same lines. Only it's not about printing characters, and whether these characters should be underlined, *italic* or **bold**. It's about which notes should be played, for how long, how loudly, and which effects are to be used.

Protocol

MIDI signals are all about *events*. The pressing down of a key is an event, as is the velocity with which it's done, the releasing of the key, the choice of sound, and the use of your pedals. All these events are turned into MIDI codes. All manufacturers use the same codes for the same events, so instruments are able to 'talk' to each other. Actually, MIDI is little more than a series of manufacturers' agreements (known as *the MIDI protocol*) on how instruments are supposed to understand each other.

Channels

Electronic instruments have many sounds, and quite a few of them can be used simultaneously. Take home keyboards as an example. Accompaniments have a lot of different sounds going on at the same time, and on top of that there's room for you to add a solo or a melody. MIDI allows you to add even more sounds. How about an extra synth part, or adding extra sounds to the accompaniments? For every single purpose, MIDI has a separate channel. Sixteen channels, to be precise.

One job, one channel

Every one of these sixteen MIDI channels can be given a different job to do. It is pretty much standard to use channel 10 for drums. An external synth would be given a different channel. If this should be a multitimbral instrument (see page 47), you would need to assign a different channel to each sound you wanted to use.

Note numbers

In a MIDI set-up, an instrument always knows which note has been played, anywhere in the set-up. How? It's easy: every single pitch has a different *note number*. The lowest note on a digital piano is an A with note number 21, the highest note (usually a C) is number 108. The number that a certain note is assigned is understood by all other MIDI instruments. If you hit middle C, in the middle of the keyboard, note number 60 is sent out, and a middle C will be produced on the instrument you sent it to.

In and Out

All MIDI-equipped instruments have a MIDI in, to receive information, and a MIDI out, to send it. To play the sounds of a digital piano from your home keyboard you need to connect the MIDI out of the keyboard to the MIDI in of the piano. The latter receives the codes and turns them into sound. To hear whatever it is you're doing, the piano should be connected to an amp, or to the audio inputs of the instrument you're playing, which in this set-up is the *master instrument*.

Thru

Many instruments have a third MIDI connection called *MIDI thru*. This allows all the incoming MIDI information to pass straight on to another device. With thru connections you can connect a whole batch of MIDI instruments to one other, a technique known as *daisy-chaining*.

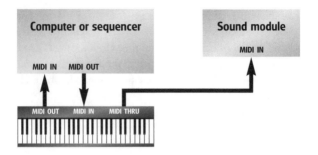

Local off

MIDI is also used to control the sound your instrument itself produces. The signals from the keys themselves are turned into MIDI codes and sent to the internal sound-generating part of your instrument – much as would be the case when using an external sound module. Sometimes it's useful to be able to disconnect the internal sound generator from the instrument's keyboard. For example, you might want to play the sounds of an external synth from a home keyboard without hearing the keyboard's own sounds. To do this, you switch the keyboard to MIDI *local off*; by doing so you simply turn off the local, internal MIDI-connection. *Local on* lets you use the internal sounds again.

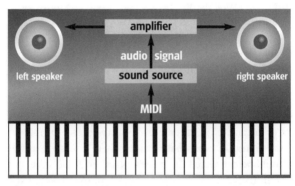

With local on, the keys trigger MIDI signals that drive the sound source, in turn producing an audio signal amplified by the amp and speakers

OTHER MIDI DEVICES

Besides keyboards, pianos and synthesizers there are quite a few other devices that have MIDI. Strictly speaking, these devices are not musical instruments, because you can't play them directly. You can play *with* them however, in many, many ways. Sound modules, sequencers and computers are the commonest examples.

MIDI modules

If you want to expand the capabilities of your instrument, you can get yourself an external MIDI module. There are keyboard, synthesizer and piano modules (basically the instrument minus the keys), but also modules containing bass, percussion or guitar sounds, mixtures of any of these, or even a full range of accompaniments. Modules start at around £130/$200, with top-of-the-range devices costing up to ten times as much.

Sequencers

External sequencers, also known as MIDI-recorders, are usually elaborate versions of the ones found on keyboards and pianos. They usually offer more tracks, they can store more events, and they have better editing facilities. Stand-alone sequencers start at around £400/$500.

Virtual boxes

Sequencers and modules don't always come in the shape of an add-on box. There are software-based ones, too, which will be covered later.

MIDI thru boxes

MIDI-codes travel fast. Very fast. Yet if you daisy-chain five or more devices, things may start to slow down a tad. The more devices are in the chain, the greater the overall delay will be. To prevent this you use a MIDI thru box. Such a box has a number of MIDI thru connections which are all fed from a single MIDI in.

MIDI patch bays

The next step up from a thru box is a *patch bay*. Comparable in many ways to an old-fashioned phone switchboard, a *MIDI patch bay* allows you to connect a large number of MIDI devices to each other.

Extra outputs

To prevent you from running short of channels, MIDI equipment sometimes comes with multiple MIDI outs, ins and thrus.

MIDI AND COMPUTERS

Most computer sound cards not only have sounds, but MIDI too. With the right software you can turn your computer into anything from an educational tool to a recording studio.

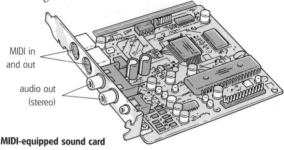

MIDI in and out

audio out (stereo)

MIDI-equipped sound card

MIDI interfacing

Sound cards that don't have MIDI can easily be upgraded by adding an external box called a *MIDI interface.* If your computer doesn't have room for a sound card, an external interface is the only option, and some (laptop) computers can be supplied with MIDI connections by using the USB-port (Universal Serial Bus) or PCMCIA cards. MIDI cards are available with or without sounds. MIDI interfaces, internal or external, don't contain sounds.

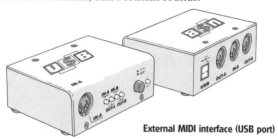

External MIDI interface (USB port)

Direct connection

Some keyboard instruments have direct computer connections, usually marked *to host* or simply *computer.* To establish the link you need a special cable and a piece of software, the so-called *driver.*

Direct computer link on a digital piano (far left)

SOFTWARE

Like any other type of software, music software is getting
more sophisticated and more affordable by the minute. And
just like any other type of software, you're required to buy
faster and faster computers to be able to run the latest
versions. What kinds of software are available? Here's a
selection.

Learning

There's a lot of tutorial MIDI software which can be used
for a wide variety of purposes, from learning to read music
to improving your keyboard dexterity, practising rhythms,
or doing ear training exercises. Prices start at around
£70/$100.

Writing

Another application is software that translates your keyboard playing into musical notation. Around £100/$100
upwards will buy you a program that aids the process of
writing down your own musical ideas, scores and exercises.

Reading

There's a way to reverse this process as well. Some of the
more sophisticated software sequencers can use a scanner
to read practically any sheet music and turn the scanned
notes into MIDI commands, which in turn can be played
back using a MIDI sound source. However, this type of
software can set you back £600/$750 or more.

Sequencing

This is without question the most popular musical
application for computers. If you already have a computer,
software sequencers have a price advantage over their
hardware counterparts. Basic packages start at as little as
£30/$50.

Sampling

Your computer can act as a sampler, too. Pick the appropriate software, plug in a microphone and record direct
onto your hard disk.

Modules

Tone, synth and accompaniment modules are much

cheaper in software form than in the usual hardware form. The obvious drawback? You have to lug your computer around if you go out and play somewhere – and most computers were not built for that purpose.

Names to look for
Software sequencing packages widely vary in what they have to offer, from very basic options to highly sophisticated professional features. Some well-known names are Cubase, Vision, Logic, Performer and Cakewalk.

MIDI and audio
Many of these packages are available in versions that not only sequence MIDI events, but are also capable of recording sound (*audio*, that is; MIDI is not audio). Sounds interesting? Then get yourself the fastest computer you can buy, and make sure there's a big hard disk inside. Specifying clock speeds and Gigabytes is useless, as this information would be outdated by the time you read it, but as a basic guide, recording audio in mono at 16 bit, 44.1 kHz (CD quality) uses 5 Megabytes per minute.

A computer becomes a recording studio, with a virtual on-screen mixing console

Your own CDs
Given the right gear, your computer can be transformed into a fully-fledged recording studio. The necessary software isn't cheap, though. Hooking up a CD-burner allows you to make your own CDs at home, too. Burners are getting cheaper all the time and CDs are making way for

DVDs already. For the latest information on hardware and software, contact your dealer, read magazines, and surf the Internet.

Master keyboards

You can use your regular computer keyboard to play the sounds on your sound card, or on any instrument that is hooked up to your computer. But there are easier and more musical options: special desktop master keyboards (no sounds, four octaves, pitch bend and modulation controls) start at £100/$150 or even less, and guess what – they're even available in computer beige.

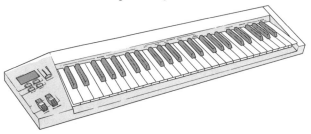

Desktop keyboard for use with a computer, featuring pitch bend and modulation

GENERAL MIDI

Practically all recent keyboards are equipped with *General MIDI (GM)*, which like MIDI itself is basically little more than a series of agreements.

Numbered sounds

One of these agreements is that not only does every pitch have a number, but so does every sound. A classical guitar has number 25, for instance, and the trumpet has 57. Instruments that are GM-compatible have at least 128 sounds on board. The complete listing starts on page 118. If these sounds had not been numbered, you'd risk triggering a bagpipe when you intended a violin, or a UFO instead of a sax.

Sixteen groups

The 128 GM sounds are split up into sixteen groups of more or less related sounds. You'll find piano-like instruments in the Piano group (sounds 001 to 008). Reed instruments, so called because they use a reed to generate sound (saxophones, oboes, clarinets, and so on), are gathered in a group called Reed, containing sounds 065 to 072.

Level 1
It was Roland that created the basis for what has become General MIDI by suggesting other manufacturers use the Roland GS-system as a general standard – what GS stands for. In order to achieve overall acceptance GS was eventually watered down to GM. It was named *Level 1*, on the assumption that a higher *Level 2* would soon follow. It never did.

GS, XG, GMX
The original GM standard dates back to 1992. That's a long time ago where electronics are concerned, and a lot has happened since. The initial number of 128 sounds, for instance, is now considered pretty low, and a large variety of other GM-related options have been introduced as well. These developments, however, have not been included in new general agreements, and manufacturers use their own proprietary names for their additions. Yamaha has XG, for example, GEM has GMX, and Roland has advanced versions of GS. All these instruments conform to basic GM as well.

DRUMS AND PERCUSSION
If you switch to General MIDI channel 10, you access a wealth of drum, cymbal and percussion sounds. Many keyboards have a special button, usually labelled *manual drums* or just *drums*, to go there directly. If you hit this button, you'll find the keys no longer produce different pitches, but different percussive sounds. Snare drums, bass drums, cymbals, toms, tambourines and triangles, congas, bongos, cow bells, shakers, and so on. In this way you can use the keys to create or program drum and percussion parts.

Icons
Many manufacturers print little icons of these percussion instruments above the keys, so you can see which key

triggers which instrument. A full listing of all the GM drum sounds and the keys they're triggered by is on page 121.

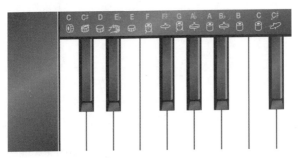

Little icons showing the instruments

Yet more

Keyboards may have more drum sounds on board than are contained in the GM list. These sounds, which are not part of the GM agreement, are usually mapped to keys 82 and up.

TIPS

- Warning: never connect MIDI inputs or outputs to an amplifier, as you risk ruining the amp.
- Another warning: always take an extra MIDI cable (or two) when you go out gigging. MIDI cables are especially fragile at the point where they connect to the five-pin plug.

10. MAINTENANCE

Electronic instruments require barely any maintenance, and have very few moving parts, so there is very little that can go wrong. At the same time keyboards benefit from being treated well, just as much as any other instrument.

A good start is to heed the warnings on the instrument's housing. Manufacturers are dead serious when they write 'Caution, risk of electric shock' on their appliances; the danger is very real. Many instruments will also have the warning 'Do not open – no user serviceable parts inside'. You may damage the instrument simply by opening it, and not realise until it's too late. Tampering with an instrument will almost certainly void the guarantee as well.

This easily adjustable stand
collapses into a flat pack

Stands

A special stand is a worthwhile investment for a home keyboard or a stage piano. The most convenient designs collapse into a flat pack for transport. A very common and easily adjustable design is the X-shaped stand, but there are other types as well.

If you only play at home, mounting a sturdy shelf on the wall works fine too. As guide to height, note that the white keys of an acoustic piano are at about 28" to 30" from the floor.

Future plans and cheap alternatives

If you intend to add other keyboards to your set-up in the future, then get an expandable stand. If you can't afford a good stand, you could make do with an ironing board for the time being. A real stand, however, offers more stability and better looks for some £25/$50, though luxury models can cost up to about three or four times that much. Ironing boards can't be expanded, either.

Water, wine or whisky

Electronic instruments thoroughly dislike moisture, whether it's water, wine, whisky or anything else. Even dregs of any type of liquid are enough to cause a short circuit or other damage, so don't put glasses, vases or any other type of container for liquids on top of your instrument.

Hot and cold

Electronic instruments are not as temperature-sensitive as guitars or violins but they don't appreciate rapid changes, nor do they fancy extremes of hot and cold. Keep your instrument away from direct sunlight, radiators, fireplaces and the like. Also be aware of the instrument's own cooling requirements; don't block up any vents, and don't blanket the instrument with ornamental rugs.

Static charge

Static charges can make your hair stand on end, or make sparks fly between yourself and a door handle. They're rarely hazardous to people, but they can seriously damage electronic instruments. Apart from switching equipment on and off spontaneously, it may also destroy delicate electronic components.

Earthing/grounding

The first step towards avoiding static charge damage is to earth/ground your instrument; if your instrument has an earth pin/terminal on its mains plug, then make sure you use it. Dry room conditions due to central heating or air conditioning often aggravate the build-up of static. Using a humidifier may help even if it's as simple as a container with water on a radiator. If all else fails, you might even try wearing shoes with leather soles.

Out of harm's way

Be sure to keep all the leads out of harm's way. This may sound obvious, but thousands of people have tripped over them, and many instruments have been seriously damaged as a result. When gigging use *gaffer tape* (*stage tape* or *duct tape*) to fix the leads to the floor.

Mains and adapters

Disconnect the instrument from the mains if you're not going to be using it for a while. Most instruments leave their internal or external transformers (*adapters*) powered up when they're plugged in, and this wastes electricity. Be sure to use the correct power supply for your instrument. A 12-volt adapter may seem to work on a 9-volt instrument, but the excessive voltage will shorten the working life of the instrument.

Pets

Dust can't really harm an instrument, but a puking cat can. Any type of acid, including gastric juices, can seriously corrode circuit boards. It's been known for pet hairs to get lodged in keyboards and cause failures too. So keep pets away from your instrument, or keep your instrument away from pets. Some pianos have a lid that can be shut. Instruments that don't can always be fitted with a removable protective cover.

Key cleaning

Sticky keys can be cleaned using a damp lint-free cloth. Avoid spraying mirror wipe or other detergents on them.

Nooks and crannies

For more intensive cleaning, use a fresh paintbrush to flick the dust from nooks and crannies, or use the brush mouth-piece on your vacuum cleaner. Avoid compressed-air spray cans. All these do is to move whatever it is you want to get rid off further into the instrument.

Disk drives

A disk drive is one of the few delicate moving parts on a keyboard. It's a good idea to check it before important gigs.

ON THE ROAD

£30–60/$50–100 will buy a padded *gig bag* for your instrument, protecting it from minor knocks and scratches. It's easier to carry around and a lot more effective than the original box. A good gig bag should be waterproof, have solid shoulder belts, smooth, strong zips and possibly one or two extra pockets for sheet music, leads, and other accessories.

Flight cases

For serious gigging and touring you'll need a flight case. This is usually a sturdy box with solid locks and hinges, corner and edge protectors and a cushioned lining. Flight cases can be custom made. The main drawbacks are weight and cost, as they start at £175/$250.

Leads

Leads have a habit of failing just before or during concerts, so bring at least one spare of every type of lead you use.

Back-ups

Floppy disks fail about as often as leads do, and usually just as suddenly. If you use one in performance, make sure you carry a back-up disk with you. To be absolutely sure, you could keep a second back-up at home, so even if you lose all your gear, you won't have lost all your music.

Insurance

Consider insuring your instrument, especially if you take it on the road. Musical instruments fall under the insurance category of 'valuables'. An ordinary home insurance policy will not cover all possible damage whether it occurs at home, on the road, in the studio, or on stage.

11. BACK IN TIME

The history of keyboard instruments stretches back for centuries. This chapter briefly traces the digital piano back to the acoustic one, and the home keyboard back to the organ.

One of the earliest true keyboard instruments is the *clavichord*, invented in the fourteenth century and in use as late as the beginning of the nineteenth. *Clavis* means key; the *chords* were the instrument's strings. The working principles of the clavichord were later applied to the spinet and harpsichord; when a key is pressed, a small pick plucks the appropriate string.

Pianofortes

The main drawback of these early instruments was their lack of touch sensitivity, as every note sounded equally loudly (or softly). Around 1700 Bartolomeo Cristofori found the solution to this problem. He replaced the picks by hammers, allowing the player to play softly (*piano*, in Italian) as well as loudly (*forte*). The instrument's name? The *Pianoforte*, later shortened to piano. The piano attained pretty much its final form about 150 years ago.

Electric pianos

In the late 1940s and early 1950s the first electric pianos appeared, employing short strings, metal reeds, rigid wires or tone bars instead of full length strings. The vibrations were turned into electrical signals by one or more pick-ups, similar to the ones found on electric guitars, and then sent to an amplifier.

Upright acoustic piano

Famous names

The Wurlitzer, the Hohner Pianet and the Fender Rhodes
are well-known electric pianos, although none of them are
made any longer. The Rhodes, the last models of which
were produced in 1984, regained popularity in the late
Nineties. Many keyboards and pianos have Rhodes-like
sounds on board, using Rhodes-like names to avoid
copyright problems. The sound of the original Wurlitzer
has been treated with similar respect.

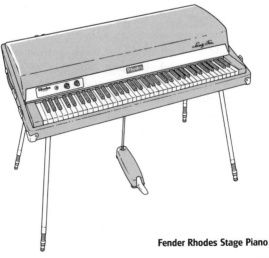

Fender Rhodes Stage Piano

Samples

In the late Seventies, Yamaha launched two electric grand pianos with almost full-length strings. They were extremely bulky and heavy, but the sound and response came closer to a real piano than anything else of their day. Soon after the same company pioneered sampling in electronic pianos. By that time Roland had already produced some electronic pianos without samples.

KEYBOARDS

Home keyboards evolved from organs, and the organ itself is a distant descendant of the panpipes: a very old instrument still played today, consisting of a row of cane tubes, each of which is tuned to a specific pitch.

A church organ is basically a giant mechanical set of panpipes. The air stream is produced by a bellows and controlled from the keyboard, so there's no need to use your breath. By using a variety of types of pipes, and then blending these together, church organs are capable of producing a wide range of sounds, including trumpet or flute simulations.

Harmonium

A harmonium, a type of organ on which the air stream is produced by a pair of foot-operated bellows, works in a similar way on a much smaller scale.

Electronic organ

The first electronic organs date from the Forties. Most of them made use of valves/vacuum tubes like those used in guitar amplifiers and old radios. Within an appropriate design valves can be made to generate specific notes. Just like valve radios, organs were eventually replaced by transistorized 'solid state' models. Guitarists never completely abandoned the valve amp, though.

Hammond organs

The Hammond tonewheel organ, patented in 1934, is no longer made, yet you may very well find this vintage organ on blues, rock or jazz stages. Instead of using air or electronics to create sound, the original Hammond organs have a little knurled spinning disc – the tonewheel – for each note. Imagine holding a stick to the tread of a spinning tyre; the knurling on the disc creates a tone in much the same way. The characteristic sound of this instrument is further enhanced through the use of a Leslie box (see page 54). Many digital keyboard instruments feature Hammond-like sounds, including, of course, the new digital Hammond instruments.

Hammond B-3

One finger
The Seventies saw the arrival of the first electronic organs with primitive drum machines built-in. Full accompaniment sections soon followed, with a Dutch company by the name of Riha pioneering a system that allowed entire orchestrations to be played with just one finger.

Analogue
The electronic organs of the day used analogue technology to create their sound. Downstream of the tone generators were filters (rather like the tone controls on your stereo) which shaped the vibrations into a wide variety of sounds, including simulations of certain instruments.

Digital
Just as pianos went digital, so did organs. Suddenly, electronic organs could sound like any instrument and the home keyboard was born.

Digital equality

Though digital pianos and home keyboards have totally different backgrounds, in practice they are no longer that dissimilar. Many keyboards now have good piano sounds, and more and more pianos come with keyboard-like features.

Analogue revival

As analogue synthesizers and classic instruments such as the Rhodes pianos and the Hammond organ became hugely popular again in the late Nineties, manufacturers started to produce quite a few digital instruments that sound and behave almost exactly like their analogue ancestors.

A digital simulation of an analogue synthesizer (Clavia)

12. THE FAMILY

Keyboards, digital pianos, organs, grand pianos, workstations, samplers and even accordions are all part of the great keyboard family. This chapter introduces some of the lesser known members.

The original family members are not hard to tell apart. Modern keyboard instruments, however, tend to resemble one another more. Also, they keep changing roles in a confusing way, as home keyboards acquire sampling facilities, pianos start to feature keyboard capabilities, any and all of them can be hooked up to a computer, and so on.

Synthesizers

Synths and home keyboards both come in plastic cases and have all sorts of knobs, sliders and buttons. The main difference? A synthesizer doesn't have accompaniments or built-in amplification, and it's designed to allow you to create (synthesize) your own sounds, rather than offering a number of factory sounds. Providing you with raw samples or oscillator generated tones, a synth gives you all the tools you need to tweak sounds into almost any shape you like.

Workstations

A *workstation* is a self-contained music production tool, housing a keyboard, a complete set of built-in sounds, a powerful sequencer, a large effects section, a disk drive and much more. Some workstations are based on a synthesizer platform, others are closer to a home keyboard. You'll come across a whole lot of different names and types, such as *arranger workstations* and *sampling workstations*.

Samplers

If you want to make creative use of anything from the sound of fingernails screeching on a blackboard to the din of a crowd or sixteen bars of classical music, then sampling is your thing. Home grown samples are stored on memory chips or on disk, and can be triggered by a keyboard.

Editing facilities

Basically, there are two types of samplers: those with keyboards and those without. Either type will usually have sound editing facilities similar to those on synths, either on board or using external computer software. Samplers start at around £250/$300 and can cost well above £2500/$5000. The sampling facilities that you find on some home keyboards have their limitations, of course, rather like the synthesizer facilities on some of these instruments.

Master keyboards

A *master keyboard* is a controller – basically no more than a device that turns keyboard action into MIDI information. Master keyboards don't contain any sounds of their own, so they have to be connected to an external sound source such as a MIDI module. Master keyboards come in a wide variety of shapes and sizes. There are small ones for desktop use in a set-up with a personal computer, and there are so-called *remote master keyboards*, designed to be played on the move. With one slung around your neck like a guitar you can bound across the stage while remotely controlling a MIDI sound source.

45-key remote keyboard (Roland)

Studio master keyboards

In contrast, few controllers are as non-portable as *studio master keyboards*, intended to centrally control synths, computers, samplers and other MIDI equipment in a studio set-up. In general terms, any keyboard is a master keyboard if it's being used to control several other MIDI devices.

Organs

Today's electronic organs and home keyboards are very similarly equipped, with a few exceptions: organs have more organ sounds, they always come with bass pedals for playing bass lines with the feet, and they have a volume pedal and twin keyboards – essential features for lots of organ music.

Accordions

The accordion is a keyboard instrument too. The left hand usually controls a combination of bass notes and chords, operated by small round buttons. The right hand, playing the melody, has either a standard keyboard layout or a button keyboard. Accordions can be fitted with MIDI. Italy's long tradition of building accordions (and organs, too) is reflected in the relatively high number of Italian electronic keyboard instrument manufacturers.

13. HOW THEY'RE MADE

Unlike acoustic drums, pianos or guitars, home keyboards and digital pianos are continually being updated with new technology, better sounds and the latest musical styles. Here's how a company might go about developing a new model.

The process usually starts off with market research. Musicians are consulted about which sounds and styles they like. Research and Development departments are quizzed about present and projected technological breakthroughs. Marketing departments investigate which models, their competitors' as well as their own, are doing well in the marketplace and how they might be surpassed.

Design

Once these questions have been answered it's time for a basic design which addresses both the outside (styling, operation, display) and the inside (electronics).

Samples

Making new samples of high quality is a time-consuming and exacting operation. Sophisticated pianos, for example, require multiple samples per sound per key, and each sample needs to be recorded meticulously and edited to fit with the others seamlessly.

Accompaniments

There are basically two approaches to programming accompaniments. The usual way is to MIDI-sequence them, in much the same way as you can on a home keyboard.

The alternative – less common – way is to bring in real musicians and have them play all the patterns, including the variations, intros and endings. Obviously, the latter approach is reserved for more expensive instruments.

Factory

Digital instrument factories look much like those that make computers or TVs. Many components, including most of the chips and the keyboard, are bought in from other manufacturers. The circuit boards, keyboard, housing and other parts are assembled into the finished product either by hand or by computer-driven machines, or by a combination of the two.

Sound

Manufacturers continue to try to improve the realism of sampled instruments. The problem lies in the fact that a sample is just that: a sample of single good quality sound. This has proved to be inadequate for capturing in electronic form the full richness of expression of an acoustic instrument. To illustrate the point, try silently holding down a few notes on an acoustic piano while hitting another one. You'll notice the strings of the 'silent' keys are now ringing as well: they resonate. This string resonance is just one of the many properties of an acoustic instrument that are very hard to reproduce electronically.

Physical modelling

One of the latest innovations uses computer technology to imitate or 'model' the physical characteristics of acoustic instruments, a technique appropriately named *physical modelling*. If you try the experiment above on a digital piano that incorporates this or a similar technique, you will find the strings of the 'silent' keys actually appear to resonate too – although they don't actually exist. The first digital instruments to use physical modelling were launched in the late 1990s.

14. THE BRANDS

Most of the companies involved with digital pianos and home keyboards manufacture other things besides musical instruments – cars, VCRs and boats being just a few of them. Here's a round-up of the major players.

ALESIS Mainly a manufacturer of digital effects and studio equipment, Alesis have a digital piano, a variety of sound modules and a number of synthesizers on the market as well.

CASIO Though best-known for calculators and other small electronic items Casio can also be credited with the very first home keyboard: the VL-Tone. Featuring ten rhythms, one key play, five sounds, and, yes, a built-in calculator, when it was released in 1981 it became a massive hit, selling in the hundreds of thousands. In recent years, Casio has claimed a major part of the lower-end keyboard and piano market.

Casio VL-Tone (1981)

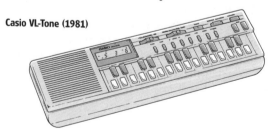

DAEWOO The Korean car people have
DAEWOO ELECTRONICS CO.,LTD. interests in a variety of other
markets, including keyboards and acoustic and digital

pianos. Their top-of-the-line digital piano comes with accompaniments and is also available as a baby grand.

Böhm Originally known as Dr. Böhm, Bohm is a German manufacturer that started by producing organs but now makes sophisticated home keyboards as well.

ENSONIQ One of the very few American companies in this field, Ensoniq is known for its digital pianos, keyboards, synthesizers and samplers, and a wide variety of related products.

FARFISA Italian Farfisa organs were very popular with rock bands in the Sixties and Seventies. As part of a general retro movement the instruments enjoyed a comeback of sorts in the Nineties. Farfisa's current range consists of mid- to high-price home keyboards.

GEM by GENERALMUSIC Generalmusic is a large Italian company producing both GEM electronic instruments and LEM pro sound equipment. GEM was the first company to release a keyboard with a large display, and premiered the multimedia keyboard as well as physical modelling for digital pianos.

HAMMOND The Hammond-Suzuki company produces keyboard instruments with digital versions of Hammond sounds and features as well as Leslie speakers.

KAWAI Originally a manufacturer of acoustic pianos, Kawai made their debut in the field of electronics with a drum machine (the R-100) and a synthesizer (K-3) in 1987. Besides their acoustic instruments Kawai produce a wide variety of keyboards and digital pianos.

KORG Korg, also from Japan, began life in the Seventies as a synthesizer manufacturer and branched out into the keyboard and piano markets relatively recently.

Most Korg home keyboards have strong workstation leanings, which shouldn't come as a surprise from a company that produced one of the most successful workstation synthesizers of all time: the M1.

KURZWEIL Kurzweil, now owned by the Korean *Music Systems* piano maker Young Chang, started out as a US company producing high quality synthesizers. Besides synths, Kurzweil build upmarket digital pianos and grands for both home and stage use.

ORLA The Italian accordion tradition makes itself felt in the Orla catalogue; as well as a variety of digital pianos, keyboards and organs, there's also an instrument resembling a home keyboard with two chromatic button keyboards designed for accordion players.

Roland® Founded in 1972, Roland soon grew to be one of the world's largest manufacturers of electronic musical instruments. They have a huge range of products on offer, including digital effects (under Roland and Boss brand names), digital recorders, synths, organs, amps and sequencers along with home keyboards and digital pianos. Famous products include the E-series keyboards and the D-50 synthesizer.

SOLTON Solton (by Ketron Lab) is an Italian company producing pianos, modules and upmarket keyboards. The name Solton is gradually being replaced by the name Ketron.

SUZUKI Another Japanese company that's known for cars – and more – is Suzuki. The company produces both home keyboards and digital pianos in various price ranges. Their Keyman is a digital piano specifically designed to be hooked up to a home stereo system.

Technics Technics, part of the massive Matsushita company (MCI, Panasonic) used to be a brand name reserved for hi-fi equipment, until a wide range of home keyboards and pianos was released under the same banner. The KN-series keyboards are well established. In 1996 Technics introduced a physical modelling synthesizer.

YAMAHA Yamaha, over a century old, has its roots in organs and pianos. Besides electronic instruments and home electronics, the company produces a wide range of acoustic instruments as well as sailing boats, motorcycles and much, much more, all products showing the logo with the three tuning forks. Yamaha's claim to fame in music electronics came with the DX-7 synthesizer (1983).

 Viscount is another company founded over a hundred years ago. Like some of the other Italian companies Viscount originally made organs. Their catalogue includes various digital pianos and grands, keyboards and accessories.

WERSI Wersi sprung upon the scene with music production DIY organs in kit form. This German company now produces ready-made top-level keyboards and organs.

15. GENERAL MIDI MAPPING

GENERAL MIDI General MIDI (GM) prescribes that every sound should have one *map position*, as it's called. All 128 GM sounds are mapped out below, followed by a similar map of GM drum sounds. Descriptions of the sounds have been included.

Some instruments seem to start at 000 and run on to 127, rather than going from 001 to 128. Consequently, these instruments will display the violin at 040, and not on 041. Don't worry: GM doesn't really read the displayed numbers, and it will always produce the sound matching the true GM number.

Banks

Some instruments have their GM collections split into two banks, A and B. A GM sound is then displayed as a letter (A or B), followed by a two digit number.

GENERAL MIDI INSTRUMENT PATCH MAP

001–008	Piano
Patch no.	**Sound**
001	Acoustic Grand
002	Bright Acoustic
003	Electric Grand
004	Honky-Tonk
005	Electric Piano 1
006	Electric Piano 2
007	Harpsichord
008	Clavinet

009–016	Chrom. Percussion
Patch no.	**Sound**
009	Celesta
010	Glockenspiel
011	Music Box
012	Vibraphone
013	Marimba
014	Xylophone
015	Tubular Bells
016	Dulcimer

017–024	Organ
Patch no.	Sound
017	Drawbar Organ
018	Percussive Organ
019	Rock Organ
020	Church Organ
021	Harmonium
022	Accordion
023	Harmonica
024	Bandoneon

025–032	Guitar
Patch no.	Sound
025	Nylon String Guitar
026	Steel String Guitar
027	Electric Jazz Guitar
028	Electric Clean Guitar
029	Electric Muted Guitar
030	Overdriven Guitar
031	Distortion Guitar
032	Guitar Harmonics

033–040	Bass
Patch no.	Sound
033	Acoustic Bass
034	Electric Bass (finger)
035	Electric Bass (pick)
036	Fretless Bass
037	Slap Bass 1
038	Slap Bass 2
039	Synth Bass 1
040	Synth Bass 2

041–048	Strings
Patch no.	Sound
041	Violin
042	Viola
043	Cello
044	Contrabass
045	Tremolo Strings
046	Pizzicato Strings
047	Orchestral Strings
048	Timpani

049–056	Ensemble
Patch no.	Sound
049	String Ensemble 1
050	String Ensemble 2
051	Synth Strings 1
052	Synth Strings 2
053	Choir Aahs
054	Voice Oohs
055	Synth Voice
056	Orchestra Hit

057–064	Brass
Patch no.	Sound
057	Trumpet
058	Trombone
059	Tuba
060	Muted Trumpet
061	French Horn
062	Brass Section
063	Synth Brass 1
064	Synth Brass 2

065–072	Reed
Patch no.	Sound
065	Soprano Sax
066	Alto Sax
067	Tenor Sax
068	Baritone Sax
069	Oboe
070	English Horn (Cor Anglais)
071	Bassoon
072	Clarinet

073–080	Pipe
Patch no.	Sound
073	Piccolo
074	Flute
075	Recorder
076	Pan Flute
077	Blown Bottle
078	Shakuhachi
079	Whistle
080	Ocarina

081–088	Synth lead
Patch no.	Sound
081	Lead 1 (square)
082	Lead 2 (sawtooth)
083	Lead 3 (calliope)
084	Lead 4 (chiff)
085	Lead 5 (charang)
086	Lead 6 (voice)
087	Lead 7 (fifths)
088	Lead 8 (bass + lead)

089–096	Synth pad
Patch no.	Sound
089	Pad 1 (new age)
090	Pad 2 (warm)
091	Pad 3 (polysynth)
092	Pad 4 (choir)
093	Pad 5 (bowed)
094	Pad 6 (metallic)
095	Pad 7 (halo)
096	Pad 8 (sweep)

097–104	Synth effects
Patch no.	Sound
097	FX 1 (rain)
098	FX 2 (soundtrack)
099	FX 3 (crystal)
100	FX 4 (atmosphere)
101	FX 5 (brightness)
102	FX 6 (goblins)
103	FX 7 (echoes)
104	FX 8 (sci-fi)

105–112	Ethnic
Patch no.	Sound
105	Sitar
106	Banjo
107	Shamisen
108	Koto
109	Kalimba
110	Bagpipe
111	Fiddle
112	Shehnai

113–120	Percussive
Patch no.	Sound
113	Tinkle Bell
114	Agogo
115	Steel Drums
116	Woodblock
117	Taiko Drum
118	Melodic Tom
119	Synth Drum
120	Reverse Cymbal

121–128	Sound effects
Patch no.	Sound
121	Guitar Fret Noise
122	Breath Noise
123	Seashore
124	Bird Tweet
125	Telephone Ring
126	Helicopter
127	Applause
128	Gunshot

GENERAL MIDI–DRUMS

On all GM instruments, channel 10 is exclusively dedicated to drums, with each sound triggered by a specific key. The list shows which sound goes with which key.

Note numbers

The first column in the listing shows the MIDI note number the sound is allocated to. The second column tells you which key it is (using the convention that middle C is C3), and the third tells you the name of the sound. Many keyboards have little icons of percussion instruments printed on the front panel just above the keys.

No.	Note	Sound
35	B0	Acoustic Bass Drum
36	C1	Another Bass Drum sound
37	C#1	Side Stick
38	D1	Acoustic Snare
39	D#1	Hand Clap
40	E1	Electric Snare
41	F1	Low Floor Tom
42	F#1	Closed Hi-hat
43	G1	High Floor Tom
44	G#1	Pedal Hi-hat
45	A1	Low Tom
46	A#1	Open Hi-hat
47	B1	Low-Mid Tom
48	C2	Hi-Mid Tom
49	C#2	Crash Cymbal 1
50	D2	High Tom
51	D#2	Ride Cymbal 1
52	E2	Chinese Cymbal
53	F2	Ride Bell
54	F#2	Tambourine
55	G2	Splash Cymbal
56	G#2	Cowbell
57	A2	Crash Cymbal 2
58	A#2	Vibraslap

No.	Note	Sound
59	B2	Ride Cymbal 2
60	C3	High Bongo
61	C#3	Low Bongo
62	D3	Mute High Conga
63	D#3	Open High Conga
64	E3	Low Conga
65	F3	High Timbale
66	F#3	Low Timbale
67	G3	High Agogo
68	G#3	Low Agogo
69	A3	Cabasa
70	A#3	Maracas
71	B3	Short Whistle
72	C4	Long Whistle
73	C#4	Short Guiro
74	D4	Long Guiro
75	D#4	Claves
76	E4	High Woodblock
77	F4	Low Woodblock
78	F#4	Mute Cuica
79	G4	Open Cuica
80	G#4	Mute Triangle
81	A4	Open Triangle

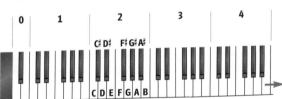

The lowest floor tom in a large drum kit is usually around 18" in diameter, and the highest tom is typically a 10". Most bass drums are 22" and most snare drums 14" in diameter.

GLOSSARY AND INDEX

This glossary contains short definitions of all the keyboard- and piano-related terms used in this book. There are also words you won't find on the previous pages, but which you may well come across in magazines, catalogues and books. The page numbers refer to the pages where the term is used in this Tipbook.

Acc. *(43, 63)* Short for accompaniment. Acc1 and acc2 are the two main subsections of an accompaniment. See: *Accompaniments.*

Accompaniments *(60–69)* Automatic backing bands or orchestras, usually consisting of a rhythm section (drums and bass) and chordal instruments. An accompaniment in a certain style commonly has two basic patterns (Original and Variation, for instance), and comes with an intro, an ending, fill-ins and breaks plus additional functions such as synchro start and stop. More sophisticated keyboards allow you to program your own accompani-

ments or adapt existing ones *(69)*. The accompaniment section may be referred to as *accompany, arranger, rhythm, conductor* or *style.*

Acoustic piano *(28, 52–53, 88–89)* Upright or grand piano with 85 or 88 keys, a wooden housing and sound board, and about 220 steel or copper-wound strings struck by felt-tipped wooden hammers.

Action *(28)* If a keyboard is said to have a good action then it has a pleasant, even and responsive feel.

Adapter *(12, 86)* Transformer; external power supply.

ADSR *(55)* Short for attack, decay, sustain and release. These four parameters make up the *envelope* of the sound: the way in which it builds up and tails off. Also known as *envelope generator* or *envelope*.

Aftertouch *(26)* Rarely seen on pianos and keyboards, aftertouch allows you to manipulate the sound by applying additional pressure to the keys when they're already depressed.

Amplification *(56–59)* Home keyboards and pianos have built-in amplifiers and speakers. External amplification helps to improve the quality of sound.

Analogue *(91–92)* Acoustic pianos, cassette recorders and vinyl records are analogue devices. Home keyboards, computers and CDs are digital devices. See also: *Digital*.

Arabic scale *(30)* Arabic music uses microtonal steps, with pitches that lie between the black and white keys on a regular keyboard. Some home keyboards allow you to play these pitches using internal or external *Arabic scale converters*.

Arpeggiator, arpeggio *(54)* Rapidly plays the notes of the chord you are holding down one after the other, producing a harp-like effect.

Assignable control, assignable jack *(36, 72)* Control or pedal connection that allows you to decide what it does.

Attack *(55)* The earliest portion of a sound. If your instrument has programmable attack times, you can for example change the 'ping' of a piano into '-ing'. See: *ADSR*.

Audio *(70–72, 80)* Audio is what you hear, just as video is what you see. The wires connecting your CD player to your amplifier carry audio signals in electrical form. The audio out on a keyboard is what you use to connect it to an amplifier. Audio in can be used to amplify a second instrument using the amp of a first. MIDI signals are not audio; never connect MIDI to an amp.

AWM sounds One of the many proprietary terms for samples.

Bach pedal See: *Sostenuto pedal*.

Backlit *(21, 46)* A backlit display can be read in the dark. Some instruments feature illuminated controls as well. See also: *Display*.

Bags and cases *(87)* Instrument carriers. Ideally, road-proof.

Balance *(43)* 1. A control setting the relative levels of upper and lower keyboard splits. 2. A control setting the relative levels of left and right loudspeakers, as on a home stereo.

Bank *(31)* The sounds of electronic instruments are sometimes grouped in banks.

Bass inversion *(66)* Creates variations in the bass pattern within an accompaniment. Also known as *revolving bass*.

Bass pedals *(35)* Foot-operated keyboard.

Bender See: *Pitch bend*.

BPM *(63)* The tempo of a piece of music is expressed in BPM: beats per minute.

Break See: *Accompaniments*.

Cartridge Small plastic boxes containing additional accompaniments.

Cases and bags *(87)* See: *Bags and cases*.

Channel *(71, 74–75, 77)* A channel carries signals. Audio or MIDI signals, for instance. MIDI uses sixteen channels, allowing you to independently control sixteen different instruments. A twelve-channel mixing console allows you to mix the signals of twelve instruments or microphones.

Chip *(5)* Complex electronic circuit in miniature form, used for a variety of tasks in computers and electronic musical instruments.

Chord *(8, 64–67)* Three or more simultaneously sounding pitches make up a chord. Home keyboards offer a variety of systems that 'deduce' the right chord from your playing only one, two or more keys. Some names for different modes: *one finger chords, intelligent chords, whole mode, piano style* and *full range chord*.

Chord symbol *(17)* To help with easy notation and reading, chords are often written as 'formulas' or symbols. C7, for example, stands for the C dominant seventh chord, which is made up of the notes C, E, G and B-flat.

Chorus *(11)* Type of effect.

Computer *(48, 50, 78–81)* With MIDI, computers can be used to hugely extend the capabilities of electronic musical instruments. Actually, any digital instrument *is* a computer itself.

Conductor See: *Accompaniments.*

Connections *(12, 70–72)* Amps, headphones, pedals, computers and other devices can be connected to your instrument via a variety of inputs and outputs. See also: *Audio* and *MIDI.*

Daisy-chaining *(75, 77)* Connecting multiple (MIDI) devices to a single source (via MIDI thru). See also: *MIDI thru.*

Damper See: *Pedals* and *Sustain.*

Data entry wheel *(32)* Rotary dial used to change a variety of settings. Also known as *alpha dial, jog wheel* or simply *dial.*

Delay *(53)* Echo effect.

Demo *(7, 22)* Factory programmed 'look at what I can do' routine to demonstrate an instrument's abilities.

Detune A facility to deliberately make an instrument sound out of tune.

Dial See: *Alpha dial.*

Digital *(5)* Computers, CDs and most electronic instruments use digital technology. All the information regarding sounds, effects, characters and styles is stored in digital form as codes consisting of ones and zeros. See also: *Analogue.*

Disk drive *(13, 39–40, 87)* Electronic musical instruments use the same type of disks and disk drives as computers. They are used to store, exchange or load songs, accompaniments and sounds.

Display *(6, 7, 8, 44–47)* Pianos often have small numeric displays, while keyboards come with bigger LCD displays, showing the selected sounds, keys, effects and more.

Distortion See: *Effects.*

DSP *(53)* Digital Signal Processor. The DSP in digital instruments is used to create and control sound effects.

Dual, dual voice See: *Layer.*

Dynamics, dynamic range *(27, 57)* An instrument has a wide dynamic range or good dynamics if it can play very softly as well as very loudly and everything in between.

Edit, editing *(37, 77)* Adapting or changing settings (i.e. sounds, sequenced songs or accompaniments) is known as editing.

Effects *(53–54)* Sound enhancers. Popular effects include reverb, chorus, delay, phasing, flanging and harmonizing. Some effects are more than mere enhancements, but absolutely define the sound; guitar effects such as distortion and overdrive spring to mind.

Electric piano *(88–89)* Non-digital (i.e. analogue) predecessor of the digital piano, producing sound by physical means.

Ending See: *Accompaniments.*

Envelope, envelope generator See: *ADSR.*

Equalizer, EQ *(55)* Tone control, much like the one you would find on your home stereo but generally more sophisticated.

Event *(36–37, 74)* In MIDI terms, simply pressing and releasing a key consists of at least four 'events': the key number is one event, the key going down is another, as is the velocity of the key (usually controlling the volume) and the release of the key is number four. These events can be stored in a MIDI sequencer as codes to be recalled at a later date. MIDI doesn't record music or sound (audio), but events.

Expander See: *Module.*

Expression pedal See: *Pedals.*

External MIDI interface See: *MIDI interface.*

Fader *(43–44)* A sliding control as opposed to a rotary control.

File format *(39)* Different types of computer and music files are stored in different formats. A popular PC format for samples is the WAV-file. See also: *Standard MIDI File.*

Fill-in See: *Accompaniments.*

Filter *(91)* One of the most important parts of a synthesizer's processing capabilities, used to shape sound. A low-pass filter, for example, is used to control the amount of high frequencies in a sound, letting the low ones pass unaffected.

Flanger *(54)* Type of effect.

Flight case *(87)* Heavy-duty travel case for instruments and musical equipment.

Floating split See: *Split.*

Floppy disk See: *Disk drive.*

Format See: *File format.*

Full range chord See: *Chord.*

General MIDI (GM) *(81–83)* Addition to the original MIDI-standard, containing specific allocations of sound numbers and channels. See also: *MIDI.*

GM See: *General MIDI.*

GMX One of the proprietary enhanced forms of GM. See also: *General MIDI.*

Grand piano Acoustic piano with a horizontal (as opposed to vertical) soundboard and strings, and 88 keys.

Groove control *(61)* Tiny differences in timing can make all the difference to whether a tune feels good or not. Some keyboards allow you to alter this, the groove, automatically.

GS Proprietary enhanced version of GM. See also: *General MIDI* and *MIDI.*

Hammer action, hammered action See: *Weighted keyboard.*

Hammond organ *(90–91)* Electric organ with mechanical sound production, based on spinning tonewheels.

Harmony, harmonizer *(54)* Type of effect.

Headphones *(6, 7, 70)* Often abbreviated to phones. The output for headphones can also be used to connect the instrument to an amp. But be careful. Read the manuals first.

Hold *(68)* The accompaniment continues after the keys have been released when hold is switched on.

Home Keyboard One of the two main subjects of this Tipbook: an electronic keyboard instrument with built-in, preset sounds and accompaniments, an amp, loudspeakers, effects and much more.

Honky-tonk Detuned piano. A familiar sound in western movie saloon soundtracks.

Input See: *Connections*.

Insurance (87) A sound idea.

Intelligent chords See: *Chord*.

Intro See: *Accompaniments*.

Jack plug (72) The most popular type of plug for audio connections. The shaft is a quarter of an inch in diameter. The mono version has two contacts (tip and sleeve) separated by a single plastic ring, the insulator. The stereo has three contacts (tip, ring and sleeve) and two plastic insulators.

Keyboard (4 and everywhere else) A word with several, rather confusing meanings. First and foremost, it is used to designate the common controller of all keyboard instruments, from a £100,000/$140,000 grand piano to a low-budget home keyboard. Second, it is short for home keyboard. Third, when a CD

credits someone with playing keys or keyboards, it means he plays one or more instruments from the family. See also: *Master keyboard*.

Keyboard amplifier See: *Amplification*.

Keyboard controller Used to indicate the actual physical set of keys used to play or 'control' a keyboard instrument's sounds.

Keys Short for keyboards. See: *Keyboard*.

Laser beams (12) Laser beams have been used as controllers.

Layer (10, 42–43) The *layer* feature allows you to stack several sounds on top of each other and sound them all with a single key. Also known as *dual* or *dual voice*.

LCD See: *Display*.

LED (47, 69) Light Emitting Diode. A very compact light-source, generally red or green.

Leslie (54–55, 91) A registered trademark for a special loudspeaker system, which is commonly used with Hammond organs. Digital simulations are denoted by such terms as *spatial sound, rotor* or *rotary*.

Level 1 *(82)* General MIDI optimistically started out as Level 1. Level 2, however, never followed. See also: *MIDI*.

Line in, line out See: *Connections*.

Local off, local on *(76)* Local off disconnects the keyboard controller from the instrument's internal sound source.

Lower See: *Split*.

Main volume See: *Master volume*.

Manual *(48)* Virtually indispensable if you want to get the most out of your instrument.

Master keyboard *(81, 94–95)* MIDI keyboard without on-board sounds, intended to control external sound sources. Portable versions of master keyboards are known as *remote keyboards*.

Master volume *(43)* Controls the overall volume of the instrument. Also known as main volume.

Memory All the data (any-thing from sounds to edits and accompaniments) of a digital instrument is stored in digital memory. There are two basic types of memory: ROM and RAM. What characterizes ROM (Read Only Memory) is that you can only take data out, not put it in. With RAM (Random Access Memory) you can do both. See also: *Registration memory* and *Sequencer*.

Metronome *(8)* A device using beeps or clicks to state the tempo, and practically a standard feature on keyboards and pianos. Tap tempo allows you to set the required tempo simply by tapping it in. See also: *BPM*.

Microtones *(30)* Pitches at intervals smaller than a semitone that lie between the keys of a keyboard. Used in Arabic and other music. See: *Arabic scale*.

MIDI *(73–83)* Short for Musical Instrument Digital Interface. MIDI-equipped instruments and other devices can, so to speak, communicate with one another.

MIDI channel *(74–75)* MIDI transmits and receives on 16 channels. See: *Channel*.

MIDI-file player Virtually all instruments equipped with disk drives are able to read Standard MIDI Files. This permits songs and accompaniments to be exchanged between widely differing instruments. See: *Standard MIDI File.*

MIDI in *(7, 75)* Connection for receiving external MIDI information.

MIDI interface *(78)* Small box containing the electronics needed to hook up a MIDI instrument to a non-MIDI-equipped computer.

MIDI out *(7, 75)* Connection for transmitting MIDI information to external devices.

MIDI patch bay *(77)* MIDI-equivalent of a telephone switchboard, allowing many different instruments to be linked via MIDI.

MIDI protocol *(74)* The agreements about what MIDI should do and how it should do it are contained in the MIDI protocol.

MIDI recorder See: *Sequencer.*

MIDI software *(79–81)* Special programs that allow you to use MIDI on your computer.

MIDI thru *(75)* Connection to pass MIDI information from one MIDI device, via a second, to another, allowing several MIDI instruments to be daisy-chained.

MIDI thru box *(77)* External box with a single MIDI in connection and several MIDI outs, allowing several MIDI devices to be connected up to a single source.

Minus one A feature which mutes the melody of a song, allowing you to play it yourself while the accompaniment continues behind you.

Mixer A mixer allows you to add the outputs of several instruments together. Each instrument is assigned to one or several channels, and each one of these usu-

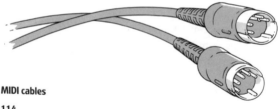

MIDI cables

ally has its own volume and tone controls, as well as a control for external effects. See also: *Channel*.

Modulation *(11, 40–41)* The modulation of a sound can be any regular alteration of it, but is usually taken to mean a slight rapid oscillation in pitch otherwise known as *vibrato*.

Module Any external box expanding an instrument's capabilities. Tone, sound or synthesizer modules give access to more sounds, and accompaniment modules do the same thing for styles. Modules are connected using MIDI. Also known as *expanders*.

Multimedia keyboard *(47)* Home keyboard with TV and/or monitor connections.

Multiswitch *(35–36)* Multiway footswitch designed to control the accompaniment.

Multitimbral *(47–48, 75)* A multitimbral instrument is able to produce several different sounds at the same time, including the various accompaniment instruments and a melody instrument. Layering allows you to control two timbres from a single key press. Most keyboards are 16-part multitimbral, a figure intended to coincide with the number of MIDI channels. Each channel has a polyphonic capability. See also: *Layer* and *MIDI channel*.

Multitrack See: *Track*.

Note number *(75)* For MIDI purposes, every pitch has a number assigned to it.

Numeric display See: *Display*.

Numeric keypad *(31)* Group of numbered buttons used for selecting sounds and accompaniments, for example.

Octave *(24–25, 29, 50)* Twelve consecutive white and black keys make up an octave, and the size of a keyboard is often expressed as the number of octaves it covers. Each sound has at least one sample per octave. Most keyboard instruments can be transposed by one or more octaves. See also: *Sample* and *Transpose*.

One finger chords See: *Chord*.

One touch *(62)* A common name for a keyboard feature that automatically selects an appropriate sound to go with a particular accompaniment.

Orchestra *(62–68)* Some home keyboards can emulate both smaller and larger orchestras (ensembles or bands).

Organ *(5, 90–91)* The predecessor of the home keyboard.

Oscillator *(93)* Oscillators are the sound source used by analogue synthesizers. The sound of a 'bare' oscillator can be shaped by several methods, filters being the most important. See also: *Filter.*

Output See: *Connections.*

Pads *(10, 33)* Series of keys or buttons used to play drum sounds or special effects. Occasionally programmable, not always touch sensitive, and also known as *touch keyboards* or *touch pads.*

Page *(46)* Because displays are usually too small to convey large amounts of information at once, they're often divided up into a number of pages.

Pan, panning *(54)* Pan is short for panorama. It sets the position of an instrument in a stereo mix: hard left, hard right or anywhere in between.

Parameter Loudness, brightness and duration are just three of the parameters of any given sound. Electronic instruments allow you to manipulate these parameters to varying degrees.

Part See: *Multitimbral.*

Patch bay See: *MIDI patch bay.*

PCM Short for Pulse Code Modulation, a term used to describe the most commonly used sampling technique.

PCMCIA card *(40, 78)* Just a bit thicker than a credit card, used to expand instruments and computers; it may be a modem, it may contain sounds or additional memory, it can be ROM or RAM, etc. See also: *Memory.*

Pedals *(9, 34–36)* Pedals can be called upon for a variety of functions. Typical uses include sustain, controlling volume, starting and stopping the accompaniments, and so on. Used on its own, the word pedal usually means sustain pedal. See: *Sustain.*

Percussion pads See: *Pads.*

Performance See: *Registration memory.*

Phaser *(54)* Type of effect.

Phones See: *Headphones.*

Physical modelling *(97, 101)* Using complex digital technology, the physical properties of acoustic instruments can be emulated electronically, making very 'acoustic' sounding digital equivalents.

Piano pedal *(9, 34)* The left pedal on a piano, also known as the soft pedal. See also: *Pedals.*

Pitch bend *(7, 11, 40–41)* A wheel, lever or button, set to the left of the keyboard, allowing you to temporarily and seamlessly change the pitch of the notes being played. Also referred to as *bender, pitch shift* or *shift.*

Polyphony, polyphonic *(47)* A 24-voice polyphonic instrument is capable of sounding 24 notes (voices) simultaneously. Early synthesizers were monophonic, producing just one note at a time. See also: *Voice.*

Ppq Pulses per quarter note See also: *Quantizing.*

Preset *(11)* A preset sound is pre-programmed by the manufacturer of the instrument. Sometimes presets can be modified by the user.

Programmable An instrument may have programmable sounds, splits, layers and other features. Once set by the user, they can be stored for later use.

Programs See: *MIDI software.*

Quantizing *(38, 69)* Sequencers record events in 'steps', distributing the notes in a timing grid. The finer this grid, the higher the quantize resolution (expressed in ppq – pulses per quarter note), and the more accurate the recording. Low quantize resolutions may help to solve timing problems when recording. See also: *Resolution.*

RAM See: *Memory.*

Range *(25, 52)* A piano has a range of over seven octaves. Five octaves is a popular size for home keyboards. The range of digital instruments can be increased by transposing the sounds. See: *Octave* and *Transpose.*

Real time *(38)* Sequencers can record in real time or in step time. In real time, the sequencer acts very much like tape, recording your playing as it happens. Step time is recording note by note, step by step.

Recorder (6, 7, 13, 36) 1. Another name for a sequencer. 2. Simple flute, a standard sound in the General MIDI set.

Registration memory (44) Overall memory for entire accompaniments or songs (RAM). Also known as *performance memory* or *single touch play*. See also: *Memory.*

Remote keyboard (94) Portable keyboard that can be slung around your neck, like a guitar, and useful for posing purposes. See also: *Master keyboard.*

Resolution (38) A high resolution sequencer is better at recording timing subtleties. Thrown in a wheelbarrow, a load of bricks will roughly take on the shape of the barrow. A load of sand will do so far more accurately. In other words, sand has a higher 'resolution' than bricks. See also: *Quantizing.*

Reverb (53) Effect. Short for reverberation.

Revolving bass See: *Bass inversion.*

Rhythm See: *Accompaniments.*

Rhythm piano (5) Digital piano with built-in accompaniments.

Ribbon (12, 40) A ribbon controller is operated by sliding a finger over it to control any one of a number of effects.

ROM See: *Memory.*

Rotor, rotary Type of effect. See also: *Leslie.*

Sample (5, 39, 49–51, 79, 94, 96) Digitally recorded sound; home keyboards and digital pianos use samples as their sound source.

Sampler (94) A device to record, manipulate and play back samples. See also: *Sample.*

Scale tuning (29–30) Type of piano tuning. See also: *Arabic scale* and *Tuning.*

Sequencer (13, 36–38, 77, 79) Digital recorder of electronic, musical events, as opposed to a recorder of sounds. Sequencers can come built into instruments, but they're also available separately, either as a standalone box or as computer software. Also known as *recorder* or (external) *MIDI recorder*. See: *Event*.

Single touch play See: *Registration memory*.

SMF See: *Standard MIDI File*.

Soft keys *(32)* Control buttons on the perimeter of an LCD, used to select items from information in the display. Their exact functions change along with the information shown.

Sostenuto pedal *(35)* Not a very common pedal, found on some acoustic pianos. Also known as *Steinway pedal* or *Bach pedal*.

Sound card Pretty much every personal computer has one, allowing it to be incorporated in a music set-up. It may be able to deal with MIDI information. See also: *MIDI card*.

Spatial sound Type of effect. See also: *Leslie*.

Split *(6, 9, 29, 41–42)* Organs often have upper and lower keyboards, so that you can play two different sounds at the same time. The keyboard of home keyboards and digital pianos can be 'split' for the same purpose. If you have a *floating split*, you can position the split anywhere you like. The left-hand and right-hand sides are indicated by 'lower' and 'upper' respectively. Some instruments offer more splits.

Stage piano *(5, 21, 59)* Digital piano, specially designed for live use.

Stand *(84–85)* Most keyboard stands are of the X-shaped variety, but other models do exist.

Standard MIDI File *(39, 73)* A sequencer file conforming to the General MIDI standard. All GM instruments will be able to read this file type via their own sequencers or a suitable external type. See also: *General MIDI* and *MIDI-file player*.

Static charge *(85)* A mere annoyance for humans, but a major liability to electronic instruments, as it can damage circuitry.

Steinway pedal See: *Pedals* and *Sostenuto pedal*.

Step time See: *Real time*.

Stereo *(71)* You can use a standard home stereo to amplify your instrument, but be careful, and read the appropriate manuals in advance. See: *Connections.*

Style 1. Type of music. 2. Accompaniment pattern. See: *Accompaniments.*

Sustain *(9, 34)* Using a sustain pedal allows you to let notes ring on even though the keys are not depressed. Also known as: *pedal, damper* or *damper pedal.* See also: *Pedals.*

Synchro start and stop See: *Accompaniments.*

Synthesizer *(12, 49, 55, 93)* Electronic musical instrument designed to create, manipulate and program sounds.

Synthesizer module Synthesizer without a keyboard, designed to be controlled externally, usually via MIDI. See: *Module* and *Synthesizer.*

Tap tempo See: *Metronome.*

Tempo *(62–63)* The speed of a piece of music. See also: *BPM* and *Metronome.*

Timbre French word (pronounced 'tamber') which normally means tone or tone colour. In the context of electronic instruments timbre usually means simply sound. See: *Multitimbral.*

Touch keyboard See: *Pads.*

Touch sensitivity *(9, 26)* An instrument with a touch sensitive keyboard sounds louder the harder you strike the keys, and vice versa. Also referred to as *touch response* and *velocity.* Velocity actually means speed; the instrument measures the speed at which the touch sensitive key is sent downwards.

Track *(37–38, 63)* Each part of an accompaniment is assigned to a separate track. Sophisticated sequencers have multiple tracks to allow several parts to be recorded independently of each other and played back simultaneously (multitracking).

Transpose *(29)* By transposing an instrument's pitch, you can make it sound higher or lower (in halftone steps, up to one or more octaves). See: *Octave* and *Tuning.*

Tuning *(29–30)* Most instruments can have their

overall pitch finely adjusted up or down a small amount. Some digital pianos can be tuned key by key just like acoustic ones.

Used instruments *(23)* How to buy one.

Variation Minor preset alteration of a basic sound *(30, 32–33)*, accompaniment or fill *(67–68)*. See also: *Accompaniments.*

Velocity See: *Touch sensitivity.*

Vibrato See: *Modulation.*

Voice Every note you play constitutes a voice. A 64-voice instrument allows you to play 64 notes at the same time. When playing a C major chord, the notes C, E, G use up three voices. Playing this same chord using layering would take at least six voices. A keyboard at full steam (accompaniments, solo and additional sounds) uses up more

voices than you might think. See also: *Layer, Polyphony* and *Timbre.*

Volume *(43–44)* Most instruments allow you to set the volume levels of each individual sound, as well as the overall instrument's level.

Volume pedal See: *Pedals.*

WAV-file See: *File format.*

Weighted keyboard *(28)* A keyboard with a feel like that of a real acoustic piano using moving hammers, which is why it's also known as a *hammer action* or *hammered action keyboard.*

Workstation *(93)* A musical Swiss Army knife: a keyboard instrument with sounds, sequencer, effects and many other features all rolled into one.

XG Proprietary enhancement of GM. See also: *General MIDI.*

WANT TO KNOW MORE?

This book gives you all the basics you need for buying, maintaining and using a keyboard or a digital piano. If you want to know more, try the magazines, books, Web sites and newsgroups listed below

MAGAZINES

North American and international magazines

- *Keyboard*, phone (800) 289-9919 or (785) 841-1631, www.keyboardmag.com
- *Music & Computers*, www.music-and-computers.com
- *Keyboard Companion*, phone (310) 474-8966, fax (310) 475-0092, www.keyboardcompanion.com (NB future publication in doubt as of Feb 2000)
- *Piano & Keyboard*, fax (415) 458-2955, www.pianoandkeyboard.com

BRITISH MAGAZINES

- *Future Music*, phone 01225 442244, fax 01225 732282, www.futuremusic.com
- *Sound On Sound*, phone 01954 789888, fax 01954 789895, www.sospubs.co.uk
- *Keyboard Player*, phone 020 83672938, fax 020 83672359, www.keyboardplayer.com

THE INTERNET

The Internet contains vast amounts of information on keyboards, pianos, modules and other digital musician's equipment. A lot of the sites have been set up by shops or manufacturers, but there are also many independently run sites. A manufacturer's Web site address (URL) often has the form www.[brand].com where [brand] is the appropriate brand name. If you want to have a look around, visit one of the many search engines and use something like home + keyboard or digital + piano as a search string.

BOOKS

There are few books dedicated to home keyboards and digital pianos, but there are many titles on a wide variety of related subjects. MIDI, sampling, synthesizers, and music and computers are the most popular ones.

ESSENTIAL DATA

In the event of your equipment being stolen or lost, or if you decide to sell it, it's useful to have all relevant data at hand. Here's two pages to make those notes. For the insurance, for the police or just for yourself.

INSURANCE

Company:

Phone: Fax:

Agent:

Phone: Fax:

Policy number:

Premium:

INSTRUMENTS AND ACCESSORIES

Make and model:

Serial number:

Value:

Specifications:

Date of purchase:

Dealer:

Phone: Fax:

Make and model:

Serial number:

Value:

Specifications:

Date of purchase:

Dealer:

Phone: Fax:

Make and model:

Serial number:

Value:

Specifications:

Date of purchase:

Dealer:

Phone: Fax:

ADDITIONAL NOTES

....
....
....
....
....
....
....
....
....
....
....
....
....
....
....
....
....
....
....
....
....
....

ADDITIONAL NOTES

....
....
....
....
....
....
....
....
....
....
....
....
....
....
....
....
....
....
....
....
....
....
....
....
....
....
....
....
....
....